"*Screenwriting for Teens* is quite simply the crown jewel of scr[...] ring, accessible, practical instruction book for fundamentals. Author/screenwriter Christina Hamlett takes y[...] ference book for the more experienced writer basics of screenwriting and dissects them to the fundamental[...] *[...]ing for Teens* is an excellent textbook for teaching with passion, wit, and good old-fashioned common sense, th[...] lls of screenwriting, in easily digested morsels of every screenwriting amateur and veteran wanting to read, hi[...] a professional." it over and over again!"
    — Cynthia Brohas-Gulacsy, Talent Manager/Screen[...] [...]nsultant, award-winning Producer/Director and [...]*: How to Write and Create Characters Using the [...]of Motivation*

"In this fact-packed book, Christina Hamlett strips away the [...] leaves any screenwriter — teen or no teen — a cut-to-the-ch[...] *[...]for Teens* is a brilliant and logical step-by-step writing and compelling storytelling. If you're a teenager thin[...] er as well as a must-have manual for the seasoned a career, read this book or you're grounded!" *[...]for Teens* is a must for every high school, college
    — Jeff Maxwell, Actor (*M*A*S*H*), Director, Produc[...] Hamlett's publication is a wealth of information [...]ll writers need to know, or be reminded of!"

"What a terrific book! The material is comprehensive and pe[...] [...]inning Playwright (*And Learn to Fly, The Metro* audience, and the writing style combines information with h[...] *[...]land: A Thriller*) and Filmmaker (*Softer Than the* helpful are the links for further information, including free [...] *of an All-American Jock, The Beach*) Highly recommended for purchase in high school and publi[...]
    — Susan Hodge, Librarian, Flintridge Preparato[...] [...]y text like this one that uses students' interest in La Canada, CA [...]nd to understand and appreciate how scripts are

"Christina Hamlett's book *Screenwriting for Teens* is a ma[...] [...]ff, former ABC Programming Executive, ness. Always simple, never simplistic: Complex topics are[...] [...]adio, TV & Film Department, California State level that today's sophisticated teens can easily understan[...] condescension. *Screenwriting for Teens* shows a keen unde[...] of screenwriting and of the unique needs of the audience [...] [...] full of valuable lessons and specially-designed recommend it highly for anyone — teen or adult — who [...] [...] inspire and motivate young screenwriters at 'making movies,' but to create quality, cinematic art." [...]pts tackle everything from formatting and
    — Robert Parker, MM, DMA (high-school teac[...] [...]ts and conquering writers block. Also an extra-[...] f useful books, websites and other scripting

"Wow! A gift to every aspiring young filmmaker. Read th[...] your story, develop compelling characters, and avoid the[...] [...]Script Consultant, Co-Executive Producer and years to correct." *[...]elling Game: A Hollywood Insider's Look at*
    — Jay Craven, Writer/Teacher/Independent Pr[...] [...]d and Produced
    (*Where the Rivers Flow North, Disappearanc[...]

"Christina Hamlett's screenwriting experience and success is unparalleled in the industry. *Screenwriting for Teens* harbors the treasured secrets of how great screenplays are written. Buy two copies so that when one copy is worn out from constant use and reference, you still have a spare."
— Jennifer Farmer, Director, Producer (*Pumpkin Man*, *Naturally Native*, *Boomerang*, *Patience*)

"Christina's book provides excellent insights for writers of all ages. She explains complex topics like structure, storytelling styles, and dramatic development in easy-to-understand language and provides on-target real world examples. This book is a must for serious lovers of writing craft and those who appreciate concise and accurate observations on the writer's journey."
— Johnna Adams, Playwright/Actress (*In the Absence of Angels*)

"*Screenwriting for Teens* is a clear and comprehensive manual that guides readers through the process involved in transforming their creative ideas into a format that can work for the screen. It will also be valuable for aspiring writers or producers who have long since waved goodbye to their teens, and are looking for a jargon-free introduction to the craft of screenwriting."
— Clare Kerr, Producer (UK)

"Christina Hamlett's *Screenwriting for Teens* is full of good advice for any novice writer, not just teens. *Screenwriting for Teens* provides a jumping-off point for young writers to make the courageous next step on the writer's journey. It all starts on the page; the written word that communicates the idea can inspire thousands into action. Christina's book can help novice screenwriters hone their skills and provide the tools necessary to start the process."
— Shannon Gardner, Executive Director, Young Filmmakers Academy

"*Screenwriting for Teens* is not just for teens; anyone interested in learning more about screenwriting will find this helpful, whether you're fifteen or fifty. Its format makes it easy to read, while relevant examples and helpful resources aid in comprehension, and will make this book one you can continue to use long after the initial reading. This book will be a good reference manual that will be relevant and helpful for years to come."
— Kari Ann Morgan, *Microfilmmaker* Magazine

"Ms. Hamlett does a great job simplifying the principles and reality of screenwriting to fit around a teenager's mind. Where was this book when I was growing up? It would have saved me years of writing in the dark."
— Matt Terry, Screenwriter and Columnist for *www.hollywoodlitsales.com*

"The astute student of screenwriting will breeze through this book of instruction and be compelled to begin a career. The exercises are more than homework. Christina's assignments will inevitably produce the next generation of masters.
— Leon Ogroske, *Writers' Journal*

"An essential toolkit for both students and educators. Hamlett's energetic writing style and plentiful examples from both classic and contemporary films make every screenwriting concept jump off the page."
— Andy Blubaugh, Northwest Film Center

SCREENWRITING FOR TEENS:

THE 100 PRINCIPLES OF SCRIPTWRITING EVERY BUDDING WRITER MUST KNOW

CHRISTINA HAMLETT

Published by Michael Wiese Productions
3940 Laurel Canyon Blvd. #1111
Studio City, CA 91604
t: 818.379.8799
f: 818.986.3408
mw@mwp.com
www.mwp.com

Cover Design: Michael Wiese Productions
Cover Photo: John Foxx
Layout: Gina Mansfield
Editor: Paul Norlen

Printed by McNaughton & Gunn, Inc., Saline, Michigan
Manufactured in the United States of America

Library of Congress Cataloging-in-Publication Data

Hamlett, Christina.
  Screenwriting for teens : the 100 principles of scriptwriting every budding writer must know / Christina Hamlett.
      p. cm.
  Filmography: p.
  Includes bibliographical references.
  ISBN 10 – 1932907181
  ISBN 13 – 9781932907186
  1. Motion picture authorship. I. Title.
PN1996.H289 2006
808.2'3--dc22

                                    2006025952

With thanks and appreciation to
Nick Morgan
whose review, advice, encouragement
and boundless enthusiasm
made this project
fun from start to finish

. . . . . . ● . . . . . .

TABLE OF CONTENTS ....

FOREWORD . . . .

In a way, lessons in how to do anything well are lessons in living. Reading Christina's wonderfully clear and precise instructions on how to write a screenplay, I'm struck by the fact that these are also lessons in life: Know what your objectives are. Focus on the important stuff. Most of all, bear in mind that what you're doing is supposed to be fun. If what you're doing is just making you unhappy, then step back, reconsider, and try doing it differently.

For any writer looking for a different approach, this book offers dozens of possibilities — true and tested principles which millions of writers in the past have employed unconsciously, myself included. It would have been nice, looking back, to have been taught all these tricks in high school, and never have to learn them again, but the weird thing is, in writing as in life, you need to keep learning the same lessons over and over.

Every time I start a new project I have to remind myself of the principles you will find here: Don't take short-cuts. Don't start writing without first immersing yourself in the world of the story. Don't be impatient and set off without a plan. Don't imagine you can re-invent the chair (the lesson of history is some structures work and some don't). At the same time, don't be lazy and just reproduce the same old stuff, but instead dig deep and try and invest what you're writing with your own sincere feelings and experiences.

Those things are difficult to achieve, and believe me, they don't get

any easier. It is part of a writer's life to despair, to run out of ideas, or worse, to spend weeks and months working on stuff which in the final analysis is mere cliché, with nothing that is true, urgent and personal in it.

Read this book, take advice, and keep applying that advice, not just to your writing but to your life. Living as a writer doesn't mean locking yourself away. It doesn't mean staring endlessly at the computer screen, fiddling with bits of dialogue week after week. If you find yourself in that place, then get out of there as fast as possible because — another eternal truth — if you're bored writing, your audience will be bored also. So switch off the computer, you're just wasting electricity. Go out and grab real life by the armload, for that is your raw material. Question, read, explore, take risks, kick open closed doors, get yourself so fired up with your own excitement about what you've found that you just can't wait to sit down and communicate it to other people.

Now you have a story to tell.

So turn (once again) to page one.

John Collee
Screenwriter
Master and Commander: The Far Side of the World, Happy Feet
Sydney, Australia 2005

INTRODUCTION ....

What are you reading right now?

No, I don't mean this book, the one you're holding in your hands. I'm talking about the paperback on your nightstand, the stacks of magazines under your bed, the sports page of yesterday's newspaper with that story about your favorite player being traded.

What's that you say? — You haven't been reading anything because you don't have time? Or is it that you're too busy thinking about what you want to write that you're afraid an outside distraction might make your brain explode?

Lean a little closer, then, 'cause you're about to learn the best kept secret of becoming a great writer. In fact, it's kept so well that it's right out there in plain sight — every day of the week — where anyone on the planet not only has access to it but can share it with a limitless number of friends. Just like a new exercise can help buff your bod, the secret of the world's best authors can transform your writing from Wimpy to Wow. Once you've added it to your daily routine, the benefits will start paying off pretty fast and in ways that will leave your competition in the dust.

It all starts with picking up a book, sitting down, and reading it from cover to cover. And not just one book, either, but as many books, magazines and newspapers as you can get your hands on.

What??? "Why should I read all *that* stuff," you're asking, "when I only want to write *movies*?"

The answer is that too many people — and not just teens — rush headlong into the process without understanding the principles of how an idea becomes a story, a story becomes a script, and that script becomes something that eventually gets made into a film. It's for that very reason you won't find the nuts and bolts of screenplay formatting in this book until toward the very end. Using a template or loading Final Draft™ on your computer won't do you any good if you don't really know what you want the camera to say or — worse — say it in a way that's not cohesive enough to make other people want to spend great gobs of money to put it in movie theaters. I know. I'm one of the gatekeepers who keeps drekky scripts from getting through Tinseltown's front door.

Plain and simple, if you want your work to make the cut, you need to familiarize yourself with the works of those who have already made the journey. Novelists, playwrights, poets, screenwriters — each of them had something to say and chose the medium they felt would be the best fit for their vision and their message. To do this, of course, they had to understand the other existing avenues that were available to them. Would Shakespeare's name be as famous if he had penned all of his plays as short stories? Could Steven Spielberg have delivered *Close Encounters of the Third Kind* as an epic poem? How many "Chicken Soup for the Whatever's Soul" anecdotes have the depth and sustainability to be feature-length films? To successfully connect with an audience, you need to know how to put a finished product in front of them.

Writers also have to possess the patience to research what's already been done so as not to unwittingly turn in a carbon copy. I can't tell you, for instance, how many times I've been pitched plots in which "an extraterrestrial gets left behind by the mother ship and befriends some little kids" or "three student filmmakers disappear in the woods, leaving only their cameras behind." Hmmm. Do they not get out to the movies or video stores very much? Or is a part of them just hoping that enough time has passed no one will remember such an "old" story?

Hollywood — and the public that supports it — has a long memory. Accordingly, it's not just looking for scripts that are well written but scripts that break exciting new ground and give movie-goers something they feel they haven't seen before. To familiarize themselves with the challenges of this goal, many writers start their film careers with bite-sized projects (five to twenty minutes in length) that show off their storytelling abilities without having to break the bank to get them produced. Through trial and error their work becomes more polished and professional, laying the foundation for longer and more complex works.

While all of the material you're about to read is applicable to the big stuff, the objective of this text is to provide you with the necessary tools and techniques to sit down and write your first film short by the time you've reached the last page. This accomplishment will, in turn, instill an appreciation for the amount of thought and planning that goes into the development of feature-length movies and the importance of making every scene, every line, and every character count. By the end of this book, you will not only have mastered the basics of story structure — a structure that applies to any type of writing you want to do — but sharpened your analytical skills and built a pretty hefty idea log as well from which you can derive inspiration for not just one film but lots of them.

Here's how it works:

Each chapter presents a concept about the screenwriting craft followed by a "Look & Learn" section that references films, television shows, books and websites to reinforce the principles that have just been put forth. The third portion of each chapter — "Brainstormers" — contains writing exercises that you can either do on your own or in a classroom with your peers. These exercises can be used in connection with a specific project you want to write or simply stir the creative juices with hypothetical scenarios that encourage you to use your imagination, start a debate with friends, or invite you to compare various films with one another.

The writing of this book actually went through the same hoops as building a script that people would like and remember; specifically, getting expert advice and paying attention to what the audience — You — wanted to see. Both of these requirements were met by the same person — a teen screenwriter named Nick Morgan whom I met in the summer of 2003 when I was teaching at Lyndon Institute in

Vermont. During the summer of 2005, Nick graciously gave up lots of his free time to review every chapter, recommend movies I might not have thought of, and ensure that every Brainstormer not only addresses the concepts presented but gets a reader's mind racing with possibilities.

Most of all, though, Nick was smart from the start to incorporate the single most important rule of being a writer into his regular routine. That rule is to *work on your dream every single day*. Maybe it's ten minutes on Monday, an hour on Tuesday, and between bites of a sandwich on Wednesday. Whatever your schedule permits, commit to your dream with consistency, discipline, and an open mind to learn from your mistakes so that each project will get better and better.

Who knows? Maybe one day soon it will be Hollywood knocking on *your* door! And when it does, I want to hear all about it.

Christina Hamlett

P.S. from Nick

Since I first met Christina about two years ago, I have done a huge amount of screenwriting and read an incredible amount of screenwriting books. This one, I must say, is my favorite. Christina manages to make everything — even complex ideas like theme and subtext — understandable, and the questions she asks — coupled with the ideas she provides — will allow you to understand everything. And once you can honestly say that you really do understand it all, you can write a really good movie.

I'm just going to add one small bit of advice: Never wait to get inspired. Set a time and every day start writing at that time, be it eleven at night or eight in the morning or four in the afternoon. Set a goal for how much you want to write, anywhere from one page to ten or more. Once you begin, and get extremely involved with your new creation, the writing will start to flow. Different days will produce different results, but in the end you won't be able to tell which parts of your screenplay were written in a moment of sudden, inspired excitement from the parts that were written when you forced yourself to sit down and write.

I think that's all I have to say, aside from my excitement about this book. Well, one more thing: Many jaded screenwriters say that you have to write at least three screenplays before you have enough experience to write a good one. That is so far from the truth! Yes, sometimes when you look back you decide you might have been able to do better. But in that moment when those words first come out of your mind and onto paper through pen, through keyboard or through whatever other medium, they will be the greatest thing.

Nick Morgan

FILM TELLS A STORY DIFFERENTLY THAN A BOOK OR A PLAY

Once word gets out that you're a writer, don't be surprised by how many people will tell you they've got an idea they think would make an awesome movie. These are the same people who will also tell you that *you* can write it *for* them and they will split the money 50/50. My advice? Smile politely and quickly run away from them. Contrary to popular belief, not every story idea, wacky joke or Starbucks experience lends itself to a screenplay. That's not to say it's a bad concept, only that some concepts are better suited to a different form of expression (i.e., a novel or a theatrical production). Here's why.

Film is a visual medium. It's called "talking pictures" because that's what it is: a string of moving images throughout which characters engage in occasional conversations that will supplement the visuals. Movies are driven by *action*.

A book is an interpretive medium. A hundred people can read the same novel and not only get a hundred different messages out of it but also envision completely different people in the various roles. Books and short stories are driven by *imagination*.

A play — which is driven by *dialogue* — is a combination of both. It provides a lot of moving parts but concurrently calls upon the audience to "fill in the blanks" of a setting that is essentially a cutaway view into the characters' immediate environment.

Each of these venues has its own advantages and disadvantages. A film, for instance, can transcend time and space but can't as easily get inside characters' heads. A play has physical limitations but greater longevity (and "do-overs") as a performance piece than a movie or book. A book can conjure any realm, era or enormous cast at far less cost but requires a much longer commitment of time (reading) in order to enjoy it.

LOOK & LEARN

A number of movies have been successfully adapted from novels and stage plays. Just as many more, however, have *not* been enthusiastically embraced by audiences. Why? Because they liked the original source material better, felt that the characters were completely miscast and/or felt that too many liberties were taken with the plot in order to update it or make it more commercially appealing. Even Margaret Mitchell, a woman whom many assumed was a huge fan of Clark Gable and wrote *Gone with the Wind* with him specifically in mind, was less than enchanted with the 1939 film. It seems the man she *really* patterned Rhett Butler after was none other than Groucho Marx.

The following websites are worth a look:
- Books Made Into Movies —
  www.unverse.com/Books2Movies.html
  (*Catch Me If You Can*, *Forrest Gump*, and *Girl, Interrupted* can be found here.)
- Based on the Book —
  www.mcpl.lib.mo.us/readers/movies/(Search for book/movie titles, author names and years of film release.)
- Stageplays.com — *www.stageplays.com*
  (For starters, click on Genres, then Musicals. Anything look familiar?)

BRAINSTORMERS

1. Choose any book or play title from the lists found at the above websites which was subsequently made into a film you have seen. In a 100-word essay, discuss which version you think was better and why.

2. What is the best book you have ever read? Could it be successfully adapted to a movie? Why or why not? Could it be successfully adapted to a stage play? Why or why not?

3. In a 100-word essay regarding the movie you want to write, explain why you feel a visual medium is the most effective way to communicate the story.

CLASSIC STORY STRUCTURE

No matter what form a story takes — stage, page or cinema — it adheres to a formula that has been around since storytelling began. This formula calls for every tale to have a beginning, a middle and an end. If you break it into simple math, the first third is the set up, the second third introduces complications and the last third is the resolution. In theory this sounds simple. In practice, however, it's not always that easy. The reason is that new writers often have a hard time determining at what point a beginning actually ends, a middle officially begins, and an ending starts to take on shape. This confusion tends to result in an opening that incorporates way too much backstory (character history), a middle that sags with too many subplots and weighty details, and a finale that is contrived or rushed just to wrap everything up in the limited time remaining.

The best way to address this problem is with a three-column template based on the desired length of the project. Let's say you want to write a fifteen-minute short. This means you'll have five minutes to set up the crisis, five to complicate it, and five to resolve it. By listing the scenes and events that will occur in each five-minute increment, you can see at a glance whether you have more elements in one column than another and make adjustments so your acts are evenly divided and progressively build the suspense for your audience.

By the end of Act 1, all of your main characters need to have been introduced along with the catalyst that sets the entire story in motion. During Act 2, the stakes are raised as the central problem gets bigger, uglier and stickier. Act 3 is the final stretch wherein the characters face their toughest obstacles and will either succeed or fail at whatever challenge was presented to them back in Act 1.

LOOK & LEARN

Witness is a great example of classic structure. In Act 1, a young Amish boy witnesses a murder in a train station. When John Book, the investigating officer, realizes a fellow cop is involved, he needs to get the boy and his mother out of town immediately. Act 2 finds him living amongst the Amish, a world that is strange and unsettling to him and yet the only one where he feels he can keep the pair out of harm's way. But wait! The villains have discovered where they've gone and are now on their way. Act 3 is the confrontation where Book squares off with his adversaries, a showdown made more dangerous by the fact that he had earlier relinquished his gun in deference to the Amish culture's strict code of non-violence.

BRAINSTORMERS

1. Another murder witness story takes a comedy spin in *Sister Act*, a film where a sassy-mouthed singer is forced to hide from the mob in an unlikely setting: an urban convent. In a 100-word essay, compare its three-act structure with Witness and explain what traits John Book and Deloris Van Cartier have in common.

2. On the back of every video box or DVD case, you'll find a running time listed for that particular film. Divide this running time by 3 and make a note of where Act 1 and Act 2 should respectively end. Now watch the movie. At the Act 1 benchmark, stop the film and write down what has happened within that "third." Restart the movie and do the same thing for the end of Acts 2 and 3.

3. What is the hardest part of a story for you to write — the beginning, middle or end? Explain your answer. How does this compare with your friends' replies?

A "STORY" IS NOT THE SAME THING AS A "PLOT"

The words "story" and "plot" are often used interchangeably. So much so, in fact, that new writers often think that they share the same definition. Where this belief can lead them astray is in planning the direction they want their projects and imaginations to go.

Let's say that your friends ask you what your film is going to be about. Your answer is likely to be something along the order of "It's about a homecoming queen who loses her crown" or "It's about a parrot that likes to herd sheep" or "It's about a high school dropout who goes to live with his grandfather."

The operative words in each case are "It's about" — a one-liner summary of the type of tale it's going to be without giving away any of the specifics on where the characters came from or where they're going next. When you can explain the gist of your film in one sentence like the examples above, you're talking about *the story*.

Assuming your listeners are intrigued with your reply, the next thing they will probably ask is, "How did she lose her crown?" "Where did the parrot learn to do that?" or "Do the two of them get along?" Any question that queries *how* a situation happened to come about or how it is going to unfold in the future is answered in terms of *the plot*.

Although these two words have independent meanings, they are nonetheless dependent on each other's presence when it comes to writing a good script. A story needs a plot to help it stay on course, open up speed and reach the finish line. A plot, however, needs the vehicle of an interesting story to give it a starting point to enter the track in the first place.

LOOK & LEARN

Braveheart is the story of William Wallace. The plot of *Braveheart* is how the murder of his wife encouraged a pacifist Scotsman to lead his countrymen in rebellion against the English.

The Incredibles is the story of a family of superheroes living in the suburbs. The plot of *The Incredibles* is how they use their respective talents to defeat an evil menace that is threatening the world as they know it.

Big is the story of a 13-year old boy who makes a wish and wakes up as an adult. The plot of *Big* (and the subsequent clone *13 Going on 30* starring Jennifer Garner) is how adults learn the importance of never letting go of their inner kid… and how kids learn to be very careful what they wish for.

BRAINSTORMERS

1. For each of the following films, identify what the *story* is about in one sentence:
   - *Harry Potter and the Sorcerer's Stone*
   - *Jurassic Park*
   - *Mrs. Doubtfire*
   - *Rocky*
   - *Dances with Wolves*
   - *The Sixth Sense*

2. For each of the films above, describe in 100 words or less what the *plot* is about. (*Hint*: You don't have enough words to describe every scene so focus your answer on the elements of each movie's beginning, middle and end.)

3. What kind of *story* do you want to write? Jot down your three best ideas using only one sentence each. What — in one sentence — is the *plot* of each of these?

A STORY'S CONTENT DETERMINES ITS LENGTH

In the last chapter, you learned how a plot derives from the premise of a story. Some plots, however, are more sustaining than others because of their layers of complexity and the amount of time it takes to address all of the difficulties that arise as a result. Feature films are generally 90 minutes to two hours in length because that allows enough opportunity for a problem to be identified, intensified and resolved.

Let's compare this to the dynamics of a TV show. Whether it's a sitcom in the city or suburbs or a drama that unfolds in a hospital, a police station, a courtroom or the White House, the same core characters return to our living rooms each week with a new problem. In the case of a half-hour sitcom, the characters have only 22 minutes to tell an entire, stand-alone chapter of their lives. Familiarity with their respective backgrounds isn't a prerequisite to enjoying any given episode because both the plot and the characters' respective traits are instantly understandable.

Your objective in a short — an independent, stand-alone package — taps these same qualities. We need no "before and after" to relate to this exact moment in their existence.

While an hour-long drama can accomplish similar results, an "episodic series" such as *Alias* or *The West Wing* will bear greater resemblance to a feature than a short because it calls upon more in-depth knowledge of the integral character relationships and past events in order to follow an extended plot. With each installment (and usually ending with a cliffhanger), the producers' goal is to attract new viewers to tune in the following week and see what happens next.

With a short, you only have one chance to make a lasting impression.

LOOK & LEARN

For each of the following TV shows, write one sentence explaining what its basic storyline is. Example: "*Gilligan's Island* is about seven people who are shipwrecked together on a remote island."

- *Seventh Heaven*
- *Scrubs*
- *Veronica Mars*
- *Alias*
- *Joan of Arcadia*
- *One on One*
- *ER*
- *Crossing Jordan*
- *24*
- *That 70's Show*

BRAINSTORMERS

1. Choose one of the TV shows listed above that you have never seen before and watch one episode of it. Who are the characters? What are their relationships to one another? What did this episode reveal about their personalities? What was the central problem in the particular episode you watched? Could this episode be completely understood on its own or do you feel you needed to have seen prior installments to know what was going on?

2. What is your favorite TV program? Is it a stand-alone or an episodic series? If you were asked to come up with a plot for this show, briefly describe what it would be, based on your knowledge of all the characters.

3. Could the plot you came up with for Question #2 be expanded to a full-length feature? Why or why not?

A COMMERCIAL IS THE ULTIMATE SHORT

Do you think you could tell a story from start to finish if you only had 60 seconds? How about 30 seconds?

Impossible as that seems, TV and radio ads accomplish this 24/7. Their goal is to sell a product or service to viewers and listeners in as little time as possible. Since money is a big factor, too, they need to meet their goal with a small cast and — in the case of TV — a small number of locations.

The placement of the commercial within a show is also important since it needs to tap into the mindset and buying power of the audience. You wouldn't, for instance, try to sell baby products in the middle of a football game or try to hawk real estate during Saturday morning cartoons. This would be like entering your comedy short in a contest or film festival that's only looking for dramas. Why? Because the best message in the world will be totally lost if it doesn't play to the right crowd.

Commercials have a lot to teach in terms of brevity — the art of making every word, character and scene really count in getting a point across. As short as they are, however, they are all written in the standard format of Beginning (Conflict), Middle (Complication) and End (Conclusion).

To break it down even further, the first half of a television commercial is spent in presenting a problem and the second half is spent in solving it. This same thing occurs when you write a script. The difference is that instead of selling your audience a *product*, you are selling them on an *idea* and a way of thinking that reflects the best of your imagination.

LOOK & LEARN

What are some of your favorite TV shows? Do you sit through all the commercials? Or do you use these breaks to grab a snack or call a friend? In order to understand how much can be packed into the tiny space of 30–60 seconds, your first assignment is to take notes on what kind of ads appear during the following types of programs: (1) a sitcom; (2) a sports event; (3) a drama series; (4) a reality show; (5) a movie; (6) a Saturday cartoon; and (7) the evening news. (Note: "Infomercials" don't count... except as an example of how *not* to write a script!)

As you watch each commercial, identify the following elements:

- The age, gender, and number of characters
- The problem presented
- The solution to the problem
- The number of locations
- The length of the commercial
- Why this product/service would appeal to people watching the program

BRAINSTORMERS

1. Using the commercials you have just watched, which ones would be the easiest to expand to a 15-minute short? Why?

2. What is your favorite food, car or line of clothing? If you were writing a 60-second commercial to sell this item, (1) who would be your dream cast and (2) what would the storyline be?

3. An advertising agency has hired you to write a 60-second commercial without any dialogue. Your characters are Darth Vader and Paris Hilton. The product is a window cleaner. Describe what you would do for the beginning, middle and end of this commercial.

A SHORT IS JUST A SLICE OF LIFE AND NOT A WHOLE LIFE STORY

In each of the commercials you watched for the last chapter, you only took a brief peek at the characters' lives and environments. We know that these fictitious characters were doing something before they walked into the scene. Likewise, we know they'll move on to something else after the commercial is over. The length of the ad, however, has dictated that all of those before-and-after activities aren't as important in selling the product as the 30–60 seconds worth of action that puts the product front and center.

What this means in a short is that — unlike an infomercial — the goal isn't to cram as many elements of a big story into as dinky a space as possible. Instead, it's to zero in on just one facet of a larger picture and allow it to expand and fill the dimensions you have spelled out. If you substitute the word "conflict" for the word "product" in the last sentence of the preceding paragraph, you'll see that a short doesn't have as much time as a feature to bring in characters, scenes and events that don't relate to the main problem.

Think of all these elements as a bunch of balloons you're trying to put in a box. The box represents anywhere from a minute to a half hour of time. While the balloons may shift shape and conform at the start, the more of them you try to add, the more you're courting disaster. Furthermore, the harder it will become to pick out your original balloon that represents the central conflict.

Now imagine that same box with only a few balloons. At any time, they are all easy to account for and are a lot more manageable to handle because they have not been forced into a space that is too small for them.

LOOK & LEARN

If someone sent you on a scavenger hunt and told you to come back with an armadillo, would it be an easy task? It would definitely help, of course, to know what an armadillo looks like. Oh, and probably also where armadillos like to hang out.

The same applies to writing shorts. By reading scripts and watching films that others have created, you'll learn to recognize what a good short looks like and how to write one of your own. The following websites are where they hang out in abundance:

- *www.pixar.com/shorts* (Go behind the scenes with award winning shorts.)
- *www.ifilm.com* (A comprehensive list of U.S. and foreign films.)
- *www.atomfilms.com* (A diverse offering of shorts and animation.)
- *www.bigfilmshorts.com* (All shorts, all the time.)
- *www.fwweekly.com* (Go to the Film tab at the top of the screen for weekly updates of new releases.)

BRAINSTORMERS

1. Just as you did with the commercials, pick a short now playing at one of the listed websites and identify (1) the age, gender and number of characters; (2) the number of locations; (3) the problem and its solution; and (4) the length of the film. What did you like/dislike about the film?

2. Is there enough substance in the short you just selected that it could be lengthened to a two-hour film? Why or why not?

3. What is your favorite feature-length movie? Identify a single scene from that movie that could stand on its own as a short with a beginning, middle and end. Explain why.

"REEL" TIME MOVES DIFFERENTLY THAN "REAL" TIME

In the previous chapter, you learned the difference between a short and a feature. This can further be compared to the difference between pointing a camera through one window of a large mansion versus taking a video tour of the entire house. We know that there are activities going on in the other rooms (as well as arrivals and departures through the front and back doors) but, for the purposes of a short, we are only concerned with those things that transpire in the specific room we have selected to record.

What happens, though, if the room we have chosen is only visited twice during the course of an entire day? Would an audience have the perseverance to sit and watch an empty room for that long? Even if the two visits themselves were exciting, funny or mysterious, the amount of real time that elapses before, during and after these events would be too taxing to hold anyone's attention.

It's for this reason that "reel time" in both shorts and features is compressed in the same way that an abridged book scoots a reader through a condensed version of a novel that he or she might not otherwise have the hours to spend absorbing. In the example of our camera on the empty room, the two events would be pushed together and all of the boring nothingness extracted. Audiences accept this manipulation of the clock because they already know that what they're seeing isn't an exact representation of reality.

On the flip side, real time *has* been used successfully to increase the agitation level of an audience. In *Titanic*, for instance, the doomed ship's final hour is played out in an actual hour. In *Going in Style*, the park bench scene with George Burns, Art Carney and Lee Strasberg poignantly captures the mindset of three men just waiting to die.

LOOK & LEARN

Reality TV programs such as *Survivor* and *The Amazing Race* set forth a premise that everything we are about to see is being filmed live 24/7 and totally unscripted. Consider, however, the following math: In a show such as *Survivor*, the participants are shipped off to 39 days on a deserted isle (deserted, of course, except for the production crew that is filming their activities). This amounts to 936 hours of unscripted action. The rules of the program are that every three days (72 hours) will equal a one-hour television broadcast. If the total number of broadcast hours only equals 13, what percentage of the castaways' experience is actually being shown to the viewers? What are all of those tribal characters doing during the hours that are *not* televised and what factors do you think influence which segments are included in the weekly broadcast?

BRAINSTORMERS

1. Identify a movie in which the story unfolds in the following time-frames: (1) a single day; (2) a week; (3) several months; (4) ten or more years. What techniques did these films use to effectively convey the passage of time (i.e., through dialogue, through title cards, through character "aging")?

2. In the film you'd like to write, how much "real time" will supposedly elapse from start to finish? If the film itself is 15 minutes long, what percentage of the total "real time" will be depicted? (Example: In a short about a four-hour college entrance exam, only 6.25% of that experience will make it into the final product.)

3. If you're not already keeping a daily journal, start one. Record everything that happens in your life (good, bad and even boring) for 30 days. At the end of 30 days, make a list of every event that could work as a short subject film.

CASTING CALL

During a recent stint as a contest judge, I read a script wherein a rebel Elvis in a post-apocalyptic Sacramento was chased across Tower Bridge by 10,000 angry gorillas. "Didn't you mean to type 'guerillas'?" I asked the writer. "No," he said, "I meant gorillas. Of course, they don't have to be *real* gorillas. We could use actors in costumes." This begs several questions. For instance, where does one *get* 10,000 gorilla suits? Where does one find 10,000 actors willing to don them and run around in triple-digit Sacramento temperatures? How, for that matter, do you make California's state capital look post-apocalyptic? Did the writer, perhaps, not read the rules that said winning scripts had to be no longer than ten minutes, shot within three days and at a cost of less than $200?

While there's nothing wrong with thinking big, there's more to be said for thinking *practical*, especially if your fledgling projects will be in the hands of people who have boundless enthusiasm but limited resources. If you're writing a short script that you and your friends plan to film yourselves, you know your available talent pool better than anyone else. To that end, you need to consider what's feasible in terms of casting. Is it a story about a Chinese basketball team that decides to operate a daycare center? That's going to call for a bunch of really tall Asian actors and a lot of little kids. If you have 'em, great. If not, that terrific script you write may take a lot longer than you want to actually get produced.

Even for screenplay competitions or pitches to feature film producers, it's always better to err on the side of moderation in terms of cast size/type/look, keeping in mind that actors not only need to have costumes but also need to be paid and fed.

(Hey, they're going to want *something* for wearing that gorilla suit all day....)

LOOK & LEARN

In *S1mOne*, a desperate director named Viktor Taransky figures out a way to reduce his overhead, create a spiffy media buzz and eliminate the chance of any tantrums from temperamental divas. His latest star, Simone, is a dream to work with. What no one except Viktor knows, however, is that she is a "synthespian"— the product of an imaginative computer program. The fact that Simone doesn't exist beyond her image on the screen proves problematic to Taransky when her popularity soars beyond his wildest expectations and he is suddenly called upon to make the Garboesque recluse more accessible to her adoring fans.

BRAINSTORMERS

1. Reese Witherspoon and Orlando Bloom come to you and say they want you to write a 10 minute short for them. They also tell you that (1) it has to take place before a football game and (2) there is no one else in the cast. Given this challenge, what would you do to set the scene and what would the plot be?

2. Shakespeare was well known for writing large-cast plays. Your assignment is to select and read one of them and identify which characters you'd deem expendable in order to reduce the cast by 50% (or more) without compromising the plot.

3. Could you write a one-person short? Your assignment is to select one character, one setting and one prop from each column and write the plot of a 5-minute story.

CHARACTER	SETTING	PROP
nanny	prison cell	notebook
doctor	phone booth	pineapple
rock star	cemetery	painting
priest	porch	skateboard
waiter	bus stop	doughnut
hiker	dressing room	beach ball

THE AUDIENCE AND THE BOX OFFICE

What if you threw a party and no one came? Film producers have the same fear. The finished product of a movie — the culmination of everyone's hard work — is supposed to be a celebration that everyone can be happy about and that everyone who attends will be talking about for months (or years!) to come. (And, of course, they also want to recoup their investment of money so they can go have even *more* fun.) As a beginning screenwriter, you're asking others to believe in your story as much as you do in order to bring it to life. Even if it's just your peers in film class, they want to know there's going to be an audience eager to see the results of their efforts. To bring in that audience, you need to be conversant in their language and savvy about what will hold their interest.

Think of some of the writing you do every day. A text message or email you write to your best pal is different from a note you write to your grandparents, a love letter you pen to a new boyfriend/girlfriend, and worlds apart from an essay or term paper you turn in for an academic grade. Why? Because you understand your target readers' expectations of the content you're putting together. Your best bud wants to hear gossip, your relatives want to know how you're doing, that new sweetie wants the poetic whisper of sweet nothings, and your teachers want proof that you've been paying attention in class.

Apply this same analysis to the script you want to write. As deeply personal as a story may be to *you*, an audience won't share the same kinship unless you can bridge the distance between your mindset and theirs. That's why "universal" plots — those employing themes that are applicable to any era, setting ("even Vermont!" Nick adds) or population — cast a wider net of appeal than "regional" tableaus that only have meaning to a select few.

LOOK & LEARN

If you were opening a new store, you'd want to research why and how your competitors bring in so much business. Let's apply this to block-buster movies. Here are some websites to help you track what's selling at the box office:

www.movieweb.com
Click on "Box Office" for daily, weekly, monthly and yearly stats. This site also includes info on upcoming features, trailers, reviews and soundtracks. What types of films seem to hold on to the top slots the longest? Who's their target audience?

www.cinemaspot.com
"Box Office Blockbusters" fills a similar function, provides lists of popular genre films, interviews, and an "If I Liked/Movielens" feature that allows you to generate personalized movie recommendations.

www.imdb.com
How many times has your topic been the subject of a film? In the left-hand pull-down menu at IMDB, go to *plots* and type in one to three keywords. This will generate a list of how many films include that topic. The same thing works for *characters*. For instance, how many movies have been done about Abraham Lincoln? Compare this to the list for Louis Pasteur. What accounts for this discrepancy?

BRAINSTORMERS

1. Go to *www.boxofficemojo.com* and click on Box Office/All Time. Choose "Domestic" or "Worldwide." What are the top three films? Your job is to take a lead character from one, the main conflict of another, and the setting of the third. In a 100-word essay, tell us how you would weave together these respective elements to create a "new" story. Who would this new film appeal to?

2. In the film you want to write, is your theme universal, regional or a combination?

3. A producer gives you with the challenge of adapting *Casablanca* to a futuristic film targeted to teens. Oh, and its signature music, "As Time Goes By", will now be sung by the pop artist of your choice. In 100 words, explain your game plan.

KNOWLEDGE = CREDIBILITY

How many times have you heard the advice, "Write what you know"? Much as you may prefer to plunge into exciting topic pools that are way over your head, there's only so much faking that can successfully float your story from start to finish. The reason is that people who *do* know about that particular topic will not only spot the holes but also start questioning your credibility regarding the *rest* of the story. If, for instance, you read a textbook that references Columbus discovering America in 1495, wouldn't it be a red flag to you that maybe the author hadn't done a very thorough job of fact-checking?

In my work as a script coverage consultant, I read lots of screenplays involving lawyers, criminal investigations, PR firms, emergency rooms, etc. While each of these encompasses compelling scenarios, it's clear from the first pages that many authors (1) don't work in these fields themselves; (2) haven't consulted any experts who do; (3) try to imitate what they see on TV; or (4) have a glamorized perception of these professions. (For example, advertising execs work normal hours, have one client a year and go to lunch a lot. Not.)

The more knowledge you have on a subject — whether it's from hands-on experience (e.g., playing championship tennis at school) or extensive study (e.g., reading everything you can find on the marriage of Napoleon and Josephine) — the better your story will hold up to scrutiny. It was Mark Twain who explained it best when he wrote: "War talk by men who have been in a war is always interesting, whereas moon talk by a poet who has not been in the moon is likely to be dull." While that's not to say you and your imagination can't aim for the stars, just make sure you describe the journey convincingly enough to pass muster with anyone in your audience who happens to be from NASA.

LOOK & LEARN

My husband hates TV courtroom dramas. In fact, they're usually enough to send him out of the room screaming "Arghghghgh!" Why? Because he's a lawyer and he knows how courtrooms really work. Let's test your own knowledge in the following crime scenario. How many goofs can you catch? (Answers at the end of the page.)

A murder has taken place in the middle of a posh restaurant. After assembling the entire group of diners and wait staff and asking whether anyone saw anything unusual, the Police Commissioner notices a cigarette lighter on the floor near the victim. He picks it up. "Does anyone know who this belongs to?" he asks. "Oh, it must have fallen out of my pocket," replies one of the diners. The Commissioner casually hands it back to him and announces to the group, "Our dispatcher will be calling each of you in a couple of weeks to get your statements. You might not want to leave town."

BRAINSTORMERS

1. What subject(s) do you feel you know really well? How could you use this area of expertise in a short film?

2. If you're writing about a subject you're totally unfamiliar with, what resources are available to you (1) at home, (2) at the library or on the Internet, or (3) within your community to ensure the accuracy of your facts?

3. What subject do you know absolutely nothing about? Suppose you had to write a short film that showed new students why they should take a class on this subject. What would be your approach in preparing the material, interviewing teachers and students, and demonstrating why this particular class was important as part of a well rounded curriculum?

Answers: We know it's a death but we won't know it's a murder until the autopsy/investigations are complete; witnesses are usually interrogated individually; Police Commissioners usually don't lead preliminary investigations; the cigarette lighter is evidence and would neither be handled nor released so casually; dispatchers don't calendar appointments for witness statements; witness statements are taken immediately, not several weeks later.

WHAT DO YOU WANT YOUR FILM TO SAY?

Every story — no matter the medium — creates an experience for its target audience. When they come to a theater to see your work, they expect to be moved by what you, the writer, have to say. While they may have no idea of what direction your story will take, they *do* know that if they come away without feeling their time and money have been well spent, it won't be *their* fault for failing to grasp your message; it will be *your* fault for not defining your vision and making it accessible to them.

The effectiveness of a message is based on its delivery of one or more of three values: intellectual, emotional and aesthetic. An *intellectual* value is one that appeals to the mind through sharing a philosophy, conveying knowledge or passing some form of moral judgment. An *emotional* value is one that arouses the passions of your viewers and causes them to laugh with joy, weep with pathos, or reminisce about lost loves, happier times or missed opportunities. An *aesthetic* value appeals to the senses, incorporating lush landscapes, eye-popping special effects, catchy music or surrealistic imagery. This same approach, by the way, is found in the design of all commercial advertising.

Think of some of your favorite movies. What did you feel while you were watching them? How did you feel when they were over? Why do some of these films linger for years while others are forgotten five minutes after you leave the lobby? For a story to create a lasting impression, it has to begin with the writer feeling enthusiastic about his or her idea and exploring the best methods to convey that enthusiasm to other people. While the topic itself can be a magnet that will draw an audience, keeping them connected to your *passion* for that topic is what will keep it fresh in their memories.

LOOK & LEARN

Where do we go when we're no longer here? Speculations about the Hereafter have long flummoxed mankind and found their way into almost every genre of filmmaking. *What Dreams May Come* is an example of a movie that blends intellectual, emotional and aesthetic values in its premise that Heaven and Hell are a representation of the deceased's own soul. The author of the novel from which this film was adapted is no stranger to cosmic inexplicabilities. Richard Matheson — a familiar name to fans of *The Outer Limits* and *The Twilight Zone* — also penned "Bid Time Return," a reincarnation romance set against the backdrop of Southern California's Hotel del Coronado. The film version is better known to moviegoers as *Somewhere in Time*. It was shot at the Grand Hotel on Mackinac Island, Michigan, which could more easily be shut down for a film production.

BRAINSTORMERS

1. Your first assignment for this chapter is to go to your local bookstore. Spend an hour there observing the various clientele and, in a 100-word essay, describe a witnessed scene that is *emotional*. How could you develop this scene into a film short? What is the message you would want to convey?

2. Your next assignment is to go to a football or basketball game and, in a 100-word essay, describe a witnessed scene that is *aesthetic*. How could you develop this scene into a film short? What is the message you would want to convey?

3. Your third assignment is to attend a classical music concert, a ballet, or an exhibition at a local art gallery. In a 100-word essay, describe a witnessed scene that is *intellectual*. How could you develop this scene into a film short? What is the message you would want to convey?

SPEAKING THE LANGUAGE OF SCREENWRITERS

Are you taking a foreign language at school? The study of other languages is not only a culturally enriching experience, but its regular practice and vocabulary building will one day allow you to travel to the countries in which those tongues are spoken and comfortably maneuver your way around like a native.

The world of screenwriting has a lot of similarities. You've literally seen a lot of the pictures, you've read about the people who inhabit this exciting realm, and you're pretty sure they'd be interested in what you have to say. But just as you wouldn't trek off to a strange locale without having at least a basic knowledge of the lingo and customs, it would also be foolish to try your hand at writing a film without first understanding how screenwriters translate their visions to the printed page.

Unlike a novel or short story where everything is described in detail, a screenplay is comprised of master scenes and dialogue. Master scenes tell us *where* and *when* something is happening; dialogue reveals *who* is talking and *what* they're saying. Within this framework are abbreviated cues that suggest *how* a shot is set up, including transitions and sound effects. This cinema shorthand not only cuts down on the amount of text on a page but shows a prospective producer that you speak his or her lingo.

Just because you can "talk the talk" fluently, however, doesn't mean you can yak incessantly. This is called "directing on paper" and is something directors don't like, especially when it comes to excessive inclusion of camera angles. Unless it's essential that a shot be an ECU (extreme close-up) or a crane view, leave such things to the pro's discretion. Your job as the writer is simply to tell the story the best way you know how.

LOOK & LEARN:

The following is a beginning list of screenplay terms and what they each mean.

FADE IN, FADE TO BLACK	These are, respectively, the first and last words that bookend every script. In other words, they stand for "Start" and "The End".
INT. AND EXT.	Every master scene is either set indoors (Interior) or outdoors (Exterior). This is typed at the left margin (slug line) and is followed by a *very* brief description; i.e., INT. – HOSPITAL ROOM or EXT. – FOREST
V.O., O.C. AND O.S.	V.O. (voiceover) is used for narration that the onscreen characters can't hear. O.C. (off-camera) and O.S. (off-screen) are used when the person speaking is present but not seen at that moment. They are typed in caps and ( )'s right after the speaker's name; i.e., BOB (O.C.)
SFX	Sound effects. This is typed at left margin; i.e., SFX: Alarm clock
DISSOLVE, CUT TO AND FADE	These are used to indicate transitions from one scene to the next and are placed at the right margin. Use them only if you want a certain effect. Otherwise, simply indicate the next master scene at the left slug line.
CU AND ECU	These stand for Close-up and Extreme Close-up and are placed at left slug line. Only use these if such direction is crucial to the scene.
INTERCUT	Primarily used for phone conversations, this allows you to switch back and forth between two locales. After you've identified the two master scenes, type INTERCUT PHONE SEQUENCE at left margin when it starts and END INTERCUT SEQUENCE when it's done.
ANGLE ON	Placed at left slug line, this is used to draw attention to a particular element in a scene; i.e., ANGLE ON Pandora's Box. Use only if that specific angle is crucial to the scene being set up.
AERIAL AND CRANE SHOTS	Placed at left slug line, these are used where height is important in establishing a certain shot; i.e., CRANE SHOT of backyard barbeque
POV	If the camera is to be used as the *eyes* of a character (i.e., seeing something from his/her point of view) it's written as: EMILY'S POV
PAN	A horizontal sweep of the scene. Written at left slug line as PAN of Oklahoma prairie

BRAINSTORMERS:

1. Go to *http://www.scriptcrawler.com*. Download and print any comedy movie script. Circle each of the above terms whenever you find them. (Note: "Transcripts" are not written in proper screen format but the terminology can still be studied.)

2. From the same website, do this exercise for any TV *drama.*

3. Now cover the right side of the table above and write the definition of each term.

LINEAR VS. NONLINEAR STORYTELLING

When you're writing a script, you not only have the power to control the pacing of the plot but also the chronology of events themselves. A mystery, for instance, can start with a murder followed by the investigation or it can begin with the murder but shift to a "prequel" of what happened up until discovery of the body. Example: the Fox series *Reunion* shifts between 1987 and 2005. Its secret? The actual identity of the deceased.

The most common method of storytelling is linear. Linear time is just like real life in that characters start at Point A and move sequentially toward Point B. Another popular method is "bookend" storytelling. In this instance, we initially meet characters after the main event has already occurred; the event itself is told in flashback, followed by a return to the same time period as was shown at the film's start. Thirdly, we have the "parallel universe" whereby a character's momentum suddenly splits into two simultaneous journeys which may or may not arrive at the same destination. A fourth strategy is the "maypole," a device that uses multiple flashbacks and points of view which all revolve — like a maypole — around a common event or theme. Even more complicated is the concept of "reverse engineering" in which the layers of plot and character are revealed in a backwards, repetitive or serpentine fashion.

The style of exposition you use in your own script depends on your audience's comfort level with abstraction and ambiguity. A younger, less sophisticated crowd will be happier with a storyline that simply moves from Point A to Point B. In contrast, those who can juggle multiple concepts and complex transitional details will be excited by plots that don't adhere to standard formulas.

LOOK & LEARN

The following films illustrate linear and nonlinear frameworks.

- *Butch Cassidy and the Sundance Kid* (linear)
- *Citizen Kane* (bookend and maypole)
- *Sliding Doors* (parallel universe)
- *Dead Again* (maypole)
- *Memento* (reverse engineering)

Another interesting movie worth studying for its creative manipulation of time is the Bill Murray comedy *Groundhog Day*. In this story, a self-centered weatherman is trapped in a quirky time warp that forces him to keep reliving the same day over and over until he can learn to become a nicer human being.

BRAINSTORMERS

1. Are there choices, risks or roads you sometimes wish you had taken? If your life were a movie, what would your parallel self be doing at this moment and would that path ever intersect with your current reality? Explain in a 100-word essay.

2. *Run Lola Run* is an action-packed race against time that is actually three stories in one. In the film you want to write, identify three different outcomes based on the rearrangement of key scenes and character interactions.

3. Reverse engineer a timeline that starts with your character taking a final and ends with what he or she was doing 24 hours previous. *Note*: With each incremental step backwards, your character has knowledge or insights gained from events the audience has not "linearly" witnessed.

STORY BEATS

In music, a "beat" is a rhythmic accent that defines the tempo of the piece being played. "Beat" is also a word used in screenplay structure and refers to accented scenes that move the story from start to finish. Within the classic three-act framework of Something Happens, Something Worse Happens, and It All Gets Resolved, there are turning points and revelations which must occur at specific spots in order to keep the plot from sagging like a wet blanket on a clothesline.

A clothesline, in fact, is perfect for understanding the placement of beats. Let's say you've got a big, wet blanket you want to hang up to dry. If you only have three clothespins, you'd probably put one at either end and one in the middle. The weight of this item, however, needs more clothespins to keep it off the ground. Take two clothespins and place one each in the middle of the two halves. For good measure, place another pin a third of the way in from the first pin on the left and a last pin a third of the way in from the pin on the right. Your placement of clothespins will look like this:

||_____||_____||_____||_____||_____||_____||
(1)   (2)   (3)   (4)   (5)   (6)   (7)

Beat (1) is the set-up that introduces the main character; (2) is the catalyst/inciting incident that will impact the hero's status quo; (3) is the first major fly in the ointment; (4) is the point of no return; the hero must see his/her objective through; (5) is the second major fly in the ointment; (6) is a complication that threatens to cost the hero everything; and (7) is the resolution of the conflict. In a 100-page script, for example, the beats between start and finish would roughly occur at pages 8, 25, 50, 75 and 91.

LOOK & LEARN

In *Tootsie*, Michael Dorsey is an unemployed actor who is desperate enough to find work that he disguises himself as a middle-aged woman named Dorothy Michaels and goes to a soap opera audition. Not only does he successfully land the part but he soon finds himself falling for Julie, one of the actresses on the show. Unaware of his true gender, Julie starts pouring her heart out to her new "gal pal" and trying to play matchmaker for her lonely father. If he fesses up to who he really is, Michael will lose this job and Julie will hate him for lying to her. If he stays silent, he'll have long-term employment on a popular TV series but Julie will never know how much he loves her. As you watch this film, identify its seven distinctive beats from the model on the previous page.

BRAINSTORMERS

1. Everyone knows the story of Sleeping Beauty and how she was awakened by a kiss. Your assignment is to write a sequel from the Prince's point of view in which his arrival at the castle is Beat (1) and the kiss is (2). Identify the content of Beats (3) through (7).

2. Scripts often undergo huge changes between first draft and final product. Go to *www.simplyscripts.com* and do a search for *Kate and Leopold*. Read the original script and identify where the seven beats fall, then rent the film and do the same thing. What differences did you note between these versions?

3. *Beowulf* is an Anglo-Saxon epic poem with a hero who does battle with a fierce monster named Grendel. If you were adapting this story to a film, what were your seven beats be?

A THEME IS THE GLUE THAT HOLDS YOUR STORY TOGETHER

In the last chapter, you learned that "story" relates to the subject matter of your script. A one-sentence description, however, is often too broad to reveal what the writer's real *feeling* is toward that topic. For a story to have a clear purpose, it must have an underlying theme that unifies and glues together all of its individual elements.

For example: "This story is about a girl whose parents divorce the summer before she starts high school."
The set-up is vague enough that it could unfold in a number of different ways:

○ She could spend the remainder of the summer trying to get them back together.

○ She could be forced to choose which one she wants to live with.

○ She could be embarrassed and try to keep the news from her friends.

○ She could run away from home.

○ She could have to adjust to one or both parents re-entering the dating pool.

Just as a catchy tune can be played in a variety of different tempos and with different instruments, this story could be written in many different ways based on each writer's opinions and personal frame of reference. A writer, for instance, who has experienced the very same thing as the character in this story is probably going to approach the subject matter in a different way than writers who are either guessing what it would be like or who are drawing on the emotions shared with them by friends.

The message that a writer wants to get across with his or her audience is the "theme" of the story. The theme is supported throughout the script by characters, dialogue and events. If, for instance, you want your theme to be that "Love conquers all," the events that unfold will concurrently challenge and reinforce this belief.

LOOK & LEARN

Proverbs are a common source of inspiration for story themes. So, too, are passages from the Bible, folk tales from foreign countries, and morality lessons from such tales as *Aesop's Fables*. If you ever experience "writer's block," these resources can provide a good jumping-off place to get the creative juices flowing again.

It is important to pick one theme for your story and stick with it. If you clutter your script with multiple themes, the final product will be confusing and unfocused.

The following websites are a good place to look for compelling themes and inspirational quotations:

- *http://www.brainyquote.com*
- *http://en.thinkexist.com/quotes/*
- *http://www.quotationreference.com*
- *http://www.manythings.org/proverbs/*
- *http://www.creativeproverbs.com*

BRAINSTORMERS

1. In each of the following films, identify the underlying theme. (Example: In *Shrek* & *Shrek 2*, the theme is "Beauty is in the eye of the beholder."

   - *High Noon*
   - *Babe*
   - *Robots*
   - *The Wizard of Oz*
   - *Mr. Smith Goes to Washington*
   - *Chariots of Fire*

2. Come up with three different stories that are each based on the following theme: "United we stand, divided we fall."

3. What is the theme of the film you want to write? How did you choose it? How will the events in your story challenge or reinforce that theme?

RELATABLE CHARACTERS ARE WHAT GIVE A STORY AN AUDIENCE

When was the last time you watched a film or television show that you just couldn't get excited about? Chances are that it's because there wasn't a single person in the cast you could personally relate to. Maybe its entire plot was peopled with squeaky second graders. Maybe it was a panel discussion comprised of foreign speakers who were all over the age of seventy. It might even have been a sitcom with middle-aged mavens who not only bore no resemblance to anyone you've ever met but who had relationship problems that just weren't all that interesting.

Contrast this to the movies and programs that *have* struck an instant chord. Is it because the characters love and hate the same things that you do? Are they engaged in adventures or holding down jobs you think you might like yourself? Have they had things happen to them that have some similarity to your own experiences? Are they people you'd like to have lunch with or maybe go out on a date? These are the kind of questions that go into the development of "relatable" characters in a screenplay.

In order to feel emotionally or sympathetically involved with a fictitious being, an audience needs to recognize areas of common ground. A story about teen angst, for instance, needs a teen in the lead whom targeted teen viewers can easily relate to. Likewise, the art of vicariously inviting an audience into the protagonist's shoes is dependent upon infusing that protagonist with the very traits, skills, relationships and dreams that the average, workaday person would most like to have. Whether it's for their courage, looks, brains, powers, popularity or just an ensemble of wacky friends, a relatable character is one that viewers will enthusiastically want to stay with for the entire ride.

LOOK & LEARN

It was Abraham Lincoln who is credited with the observation that "you can't fool all of the people all the time." Nor is it an easy task to write a screenplay that will be embraced by everyone on the planet. Some films, however, *do* come close to achieving the epitome of crossover demographics; specifically, a story that appeals to males, females, the young and the old. In recent years, animated features such as *Shrek*, *The Incredibles*, and *Finding Nemo* have provided the younger set with eye-popping color and lots of action, the adults with sophisticated dialogue, and both sexes with characters whose values, aspirations and insecurities are no different from that of their human counterparts.

BRAINSTORMERS

1. Identify a fictitious character from either the movies or TV that you feel you relate to the most. Make a list of 25 things that you and this person have in common. Make the same list for someone real whom you know very well.

2. Have you ever had to spend any time in detention? That's what happens to five radically different high school students in *The Breakfast Club*. If you could hang out with one of them for an entire day, which character would it be? What kinds of things would you do, what would you talk about, and where would you go for lunch? Could you see this person becoming a friend for life? Why or why not?

3. Who is the target audience for the movie you'd like to write? In a 100-word essay, explain what it is about your main character that will be easy for an audience to relate to on a personal level.

RELATABLE CHARACTERS COME FROM ... EVERYWHERE!!

Back in the days before I became a full-time writer, I used to work for lawyers and corporate executives. This was useful for two reasons. The first was that it paid the bills (I was also a struggling actress). The second was that it introduced me to a lot of quirky co-workers, wise mentors, dear friends and indecisive boyfriends who would one day reappear (some more favorably than others) between the covers of my novels and scripts.

Yes, yes, there's always that disclaimer that says, "*These characters have no existence outside the imagination of the author and have no relation to any parties living or dead.*" Oh puh-leeeeze! Were it not for the multitude of free material walking around us every single day, authors would have to make everybody up. In doing so, they would deprive audiences of recognizing those traits and types that remind them of people *they* know and which so easily allow them to relate to the *protagonist's* relationship to them.

Ask any fiction writer about the inspiration for his or her characters and you're likely to hear, "I patterned Aunt Sue after my Aunt Liz" or "I named the villain Petey because that was my arch nemesis in second grade." Aspiring screenwriters go a step further, often mentally picturing the actors they'd like to have star in various roles. Either method provides a framework for incorporating movement, attitude, habits and vocabulary.

We don't even have to know people intimately in order to blend aspects of their personalities into a plot — a fidgety postman, a chatty cashier, an impatient bus driver, a grandmotherly shopkeeper, a self-confident child, a nosey neighbor. Such behaviors and manners of speech contribute to creating realistic characters who will come alive in your story. (Just don't make them identifiable enough to warrant a visit from a lawyer!)

LOOK & LEARN

Award winning playwright Neil Simon never had to look very far for comedic inspiration; it was usually living under the same roof with him. In his autobiography, Rewrites, Simon introduces us to his kooky parents, his older brother Danny, his first wife Joan, and actress-wife Marsha Mason, each of whom would assume prominent roles in such works as *Lost in Yonkers*, *Barefoot in the Park*, *The Odd Couple*, *Come Blow Your Horn* and *Chapter Two*. It's not only a fun read that will demonstrate how skillful Simon was at borrowing inspiration from real people, real incidents and, oftentimes, real conversations, but will also provide a look at the kind of real tenacity that's needed to move an idea from out of your head to in front of an actual audience.

BRAINSTORMERS

1. How many different places do you go in the course of a week? Beginning today, start a running list of each one (e.g., school, church, grocery store). In addition, with each subsequent visit you make, pick out one person in these different settings who catches your eye and write a brief description of everything you observe about them. Start a Random Character File for future inspiration.

2. If you were to pattern a fictional character after your best friend, describe what the role would be (including a name). Do the same exercise for your least fave person. Do you think they would recognize themselves as these fictional personas? Why or why not?

3. If you could choose any actor to play you in a movie, who do you think would come closest in terms of looks, age, and personality? Explain your answer. For fun, survey your friends and ask who *they* think should play you.

COMPELLING IDEAS COME FROM ... EVERYWHERE ELSE!

"Where do you get all your ideas?" That's probably the most common question writers are ever asked by non-writers. Non-writers, you see, assume that ideas are magically beamed into the heads of authors every night via satellite transmissions from Saturn or perhaps emailed on a monthly basis from the Schenectady Inspiration Service.

Not so! Just as everyone has the same twenty-four hours in a day, so, too, do aspiring writers and veterans have access to limitless sources of creativity from which to develop exciting new stories. It's just a matter of keeping your eyes open... and knowing where to look.

Does your family subscribe to newspapers and magazines? Their pages are filled with possibilities that prompt speculation of "what if?" or "what happens next?"

Does your minister relate parables in church? Do you remember any of the myths and folk legends you heard in grade school? How about some of those fairy tales you were told before bedtime? A timeless message can never be told too many times.

Are your grandparents talkative about "the good old days"? Start listening... and start taking notes.

Does a certain song or the sight of a particular photo or piece of art conjure emotions you want to share? Maybe your muse is sending you vibes to write it down.

Stepped outside lately? Mother Nature is open 24/7 to tweak your imagination.

Are you anxious about college? Excited about a first date? Mortified that your mother did her impression of Beyoncé in front of your friends? Chances are that your characters could experience the same thing, too.

Looking for great ideas? Log into life. No password required.

LOOK & LEARN

In 1977, a fourteen-year-old U.K. student named Gideon Sams had an assignment in school to write a short story. He called it "The Punk" and threw it away soon after he got his grade back. His mother, however, retrieved it, thought it had merit, and got it into print. Fifteen years later, singer/director Mike Sarne saw its promise as a film. While *The Punk* may not have been a hit by any measure, its Romeo and Juliet theme just goes to show that even occasional homework assignments have the potential to yield a modest plot. (Which, of course, you can now use as your excuse for never throwing anything out.)

BRAINSTORMERS

1. In September 1954, the *Saturday Evening Post* ran a cover that featured Norman Rockwell's poignant "Breaking Home Ties." So moving was this coming-of-age image that a film of the same name was eventually made about a young man leaving home. Your assignment: Study the paintings of this American artist and choose the one that strikes the strongest emotional chord for you. In a 100-word essay, describe the kind of story you would write involving the people depicted.

2. Lots of William Shakespeare's plays have been adapted to movies. How many of them can you list? Which ones were the most successful at the box office? Why?

3. I call this next exercise "Food for Thought." Take a cookbook and open it to any random page. Study whatever recipe is described and/or illustrated on that page. Your assignment is to write a 100-word fictitious essay describing (1) who is going to be cooking this dish; (2) who he or she is cooking it for; (3) whether it is an everyday meal or a special occasion; (4) where it will be served; and (5) what is going to go wrong before, during or after this meal.

IDEAS THAT WORK BEST AS SHORTS

Ideas that lend themselves well to shorts are those in which a hero wants/needs to move from Point A to Point B but is diverted by Point C. This interruption will either take him in an alternative direction (Point D) or reinforce his desire to reach his original goal.

Example: Joe wants to take Bonnie to the dance. Alex asks her first. This forces Joe to either ask someone else or persevere in the hope Bonnie will change her mind. Joe has no other issues, goals or objectives.

This simplistic plot can be told with three people (two if you omit Alex), one set (a hallway or front door), and very little time (three to fifteen minutes). In spite of a short's brief duration, a writer can incorporate symbolism, ambiguity and ellipses (jumps in time) that viewers will more readily accept than if it were presented to them in a longer form.

Global issues that are expressed in a personal context work well as shorts, too.

Example: Samantha is reading a letter from her older brother who is excited to be coming back from Iraq and seeing his wife and newborn son. She looks up at the camera and tells us that he was killed in an ambush the day before his flight home.

In the minimalist fashion above, the writer's intention to express an opinion, mood, or philosophy says much more than a full-scale production and at a much lower cost.

The third candidate for shorts is a joke or personal experience that isn't of sufficient depth — or integral to a larger conflict — to hold an audience's attention beyond the punch line. These are also played out within a very short timeframe.

Example: Mr. Gilliam, the math teacher, always stomps the top of his wastebasket when it gets too full. Jerry and Clyde fill it with water and float some crumpled papers on top just before he gets to class.

While humorous scenes such as this could be incorporated as a vignette in a feature-length film, the short itself needs to be a standalone product to be successful.

LOOK & LEARN

One-act stage plays are the theatrical equivalent of film shorts. These typically utilize a single set, a short timeframe (e.g., an afternoon), and just enough characters necessary to deliver the plot. Transitions are handled through creative lighting, music and/or short vignettes played in front of the curtain. To familiarize yourself with the similarities between one-acts and shorts, visit *www.playsmag.com*, the website of Plays, "the Drama Magazine for Young People." Sample scripts for study can be individually downloaded as Adobe Acrobat files. In addition, Plays publishes a monthly magazine of original scripts as well as collections of one-act productions targeted to different age groups, holidays, and cultural/historical experiences.

BRAINSTORMERS

1. Select and read an original play script from the Plays website. In a 100-word essay, discuss whether it is a single-issue conflict, a moral/philosophical platform, or a one joke/slice-of-life vignette. Could this premise be expanded to a longer work? Why or why not?

2. On the preceding page, you had the premise of Joe wanting to take Bonnie as his date to the upcoming dance. If you were only allowed to use one character and one setting to tell this story, who would it be and what would you use as your backdrop?

3. What issue in life do you feel most strongly about? If you were using a fifteen-minute short as a vehicle to communicate your feelings about this subject to an audience, who would your characters be, what would be your central location, and how would you use the medium of film to communicate your passion?

A CONFLICT IS WHAT DRIVES A PLOT FORWARD

What would life be like if you didn't have any problems? What if there were no consequences to playing video games all day instead of studying for your algebra test? What if you never had to compete in order to make the varsity baseball team? What if the people around you always said "yes" to whatever you wanted them to do?

While there's not a person among us who wouldn't like a stress-free day now and then, a lifetime of it would probably get mind-numbingly boring a lot faster than you'd think. It's the angst, the fears and the occasional failures that test our mettle and enable us to rise above our perceived limitations. In other words, it's the *conflict* that not only keeps life worth experiencing but makes the rewards worth the fight.

The same thing is true of films, regardless of their length. A story about "friends just hanging out" in the parking lot may mirror after-school reality. Reality, however, isn't what movie magic is all about. People watch movies to see things *happen* in the context of problem and solution. The bigger the problem and the more at stake for the characters, the more compelling that movie will be. Unlike Jerry and George in *Seinfeld* who fashioned an entire season around a show about *nothing*, movies need to be about *something* to keep our attention.

For a conflict to be compelling, it needs to meet the following criteria:

1. It has to be a problem that the members of the audience can relate to.

2. The opposition has to be as strong as the efforts of pursuit.

3. It has to be a problem of sufficient weight that it requires more than one conversation to resolve it.

LOOK & LEARN

In *Robin Hood, Prince of Thieves*, the Sheriff of Nottingham has let power and greed go to his head. While noble King Richard is off fighting in the Crusades, the Sheriff is orchestrating an alliance with the barons and robbing the poor. Enter Robin Hood who decides that robbing the rich is a much better idea to restore balance to Richard's kingdom. His quest for justice is *relatable to audiences* because everyone — at some point in their lives — has been victimized by a bully. By training the men of Sherwood Forest to become fighters, he *poses a formidable threat* to the Sheriff's plans. Lastly, the intensity of Robin and the Sheriff's *conflict can't be resolved in one chat* over a cup of latte. The presence of these three critical components all drive the plot forward.

BRAINSTORMERS

1. In the film that you plan to write, identify what aspects of it your audience will relate to. For instance, is your main character struggling to pay her bills or trying to work up the nerve to ask someone out on a date?

2. What or who is the opposing force that will try to keep your main character from being successful? For instance, is there a corrupt tax collector who refuses to go away? Is there a wealthy jock who has expressed interest in asking the same girl to the upcoming prom?

3. Could your opposing characters resolve their differences in one conversation? Why or why not? (*Note*: If the problem *can* be fixed in one conversation, you'll have to make it a bigger problem to keep our attention.)

SHOW US WHO (AND WHAT) WE'RE ROOTING FOR

Whether you call it "protagonists versus antagonists," "good versus evil" or simply "Us versus Them," the concept of opposing forces squaring off isn't a new one in storytelling. Which side of the bleachers the audience should be sitting on, however, has been undergoing scrutiny for longer than you might imagine.

In ancient Greece, the majority of staged themes revolved — as did mainstream Greek life — around man's relationship to the gods. Vain and imperfect as they were, the gods still had the power to hit the smote button on any mortal who dared to engage them in competition. As empathetic as Athens theatergoers might be toward the human challengers, cheering aloud for them wasn't considered wise.

By Shakespeare's time, man had a new enemy to do battle with; specifically, his fellow man. The influence of the church as well as criticisms of the monarchy gave rise to popular themes in which virtue had to hold its own against villainy. Misdeeds on Earth — as in the Hereafter — did not go unnoticed or unpunished, regardless of status.

The nineteenth and twentieth centuries brought forth yet another tableau: man waging war against himself. In a trend that continues to this day, the ability to choose a team to root for can sometimes become muddied when both sides belong to the same dysfunctional whole.

While that's not to say that a modern, contemplative tale can't be as gripping as an action film, today's moviegoers are living in more impatient times. They want to know from the start which characters warrant their cheers and their angst. They want to know what it is that's being fought for and why this quest has stirred such passion to see it through.

And when the dust has settled, they also want to be able to tell which side won.

LOOK & LEARN

No longer are heroes accessorized with the white hats and sterling reputations that distinguished their predecessors. Sometimes, in fact, they're cloaked in black, have wicked wits, and an arsenal of high-tech weapons that would make James Bond envious. Such was the case in the monster hit *Van Helsing* starring Hugh Jackman. Hired to rid Transylvania once and for all of its undead residents, Van Helsing gives us dialogue that flirts with his own moral ambiguity.

> *Anna Valerious*: Some say you're a murderer,
> Mr. Van Helsing. Others say you're a holy
> man. Which is it?

> *Van Helsing*: It's a bit of both, I think.

While the rise of "anti-heroes" such as *Van Helsing* and *Constantine* may seem new, they actually use the same formula of good versus evil. The only difference is that the evil faction is even *more* vile than those who straddle the cosmic fence.

BRAINSTORMERS

1. Time to brush up on Greek mythology! Select any myth in which a mortal and one of the gods are on opposing sides. In your view, which one is the protagonist and which one is the antagonist? What are they fighting over? If they appeared on *People's Court* and you were the judge, what would be your verdict?

2. Let's try the same thing with Shakespeare. Choose any play and assign the characters to one side or the other. What is their conflict? Which side is "right"?

3. Identify a movie in which the "outlaws" (i.e., bandits, inmates, fugitives, etc.) are more likable than their opposition. What techniques did the writer employ to garner empathy and support for them from the audience in spite of their being on the wrong side of the law? (Example: *Butch Cassidy and the Sundance Kid*.)

SUBSTANCE VERSUS STYLE: WHO'S IN THE DRIVER'S SEAT?

Which comes first in developing a new project: the characters (substance) or the plot (style)? There are those who like to build a story from the inside out, starting with a protagonist and/or a core group of interesting personas and devising a crisis that will bring out their best and worst traits. Others prefer to work from the outside in, launching a story from the standpoint of the crisis itself (e.g., a giant asteroid is headed toward L.A.) and then determining what types of people will be affected by this particular event.

In the first instance, a script is labeled "character-driven." In a character-driven story, the protagonist is on an emotional journey in which he or she will discover aspects of their personality which will undergo acts of internal renovation predicated on good (or bad) judgment. Think of the external catalyst (conflict) as a passenger in the backseat of a car your lead character is driving. As many directions as that passenger may be shouting out, it is the driver who ultimately decides on the best road to take based on the completeness and practicality of the information provided.

In a plot-driven story, the conflict comes from external forces that are generally beyond the control of the parties involved. That external challenge now puts someone other than the protagonist in the driver's seat, forcing the latter to *react* to circumstances more than *direct* them. A purely plot-driven story only requires that the crisis itself be satisfactorily resolved as opposed to characters themselves needing to undergo substantive emotional transformations in order to deal with it. To use the car analogy, the passenger/protagonist is only trying to stop or disable the vehicle (or get out of it), not analyze whether his or her own actions or self-doubts put it on the road to begin with.

LOOK & LEARN

Action/adventure plots and movies that rely heavily on special effects and extraordinary powers tend to be plot-driven. The *Indiana Jones* trilogy, for example, provides us with a protagonist who already possesses the skills, knowledge and personality to thwart the Nazis' game plan. Contrast this to coming-of-age films such as *Billy Elliot* or *Searching for Bobby Fischer* in which the lead characters are assimilating outside information/influences and making choices that will subsequently impact the rest of their lives. Here are some more examples:

CHARACTER-DRIVEN

13 Going on 30

Dave

Legally Blond

The Sisterhood of the Traveling Pants

PLOT-DRIVEN

Butch Cassidy and the Sundance Kid

Invasion of the Body Snatchers

Speed

Agent Cody Banks

BRAINSTORMERS

1. Identify three movies you have seen which fit the definition of "character-driven." Explain how each of the protagonists in these films experienced "inner drive" and evolved as individuals between the start of the story and the ending.

2. Identify three movies which you think fit the definition of "plot-driven." For each film, describe the external conflict that had to be resolved. What traits or skills did the protagonists already possess which enabled them to respond well to these challenges?

3. Is the film you want to write character-driven or plot-driven? Provide examples to support your answer.

ALL CONFLICTS DERIVE FROM REWARD, REVENGE AND ESCAPE

No matter what type of problems you throw at your characters or what type of quests you have them pursue over the course of the story, they all have their root in one of three core objectives: the attainment of a reward, the fulfillment of revenge, or the accomplishment of an escape. These factors — which can manifest as abstract or concrete — are what set the plot in motion and keep it moving from start to finish.

Reward, revenge and escape can be defined in several different ways. Likewise, a character's success in achieving these goals can be measured in varying degrees. A reward, for instance, can take the form of laying claim to a treasure, finding true love, or winning a tough competition. Revenge can be something as simple as payback for a school rival's locker-room prank or something as complex as avenging one's family honor. An escape-driven plot focuses on release from physical captivity (e.g., a prison) as well as emotional and spiritual journeys in which the characters seek to change an unsatisfactory status quo (e.g., rising above poverty or leaving a bad relationship). Movies can also reflect a combination of these three forces working in tandem. In *The Lion King*, for example:

1. Young Simba evolves from a runaway juvenile to a mature adult who must face responsibility in order to earn respect. (ESCAPE)

2. He avenges the murder of his father, Mufasa, by the evil Uncle Scar. (REVENGE)

3. He finds friendship with Timon and Pumbaa and romance with Nala. (REWARD)

LOOK & LEARN

For each of the following films, identify whether the conflict is driven by reward, revenge, escape or a combination. Provide examples/specific scenes to support your answer. A film such as *Breaking Away*, for instance, is a combination of the townies' fight for respect (ESCAPE) and Dave's quest to win the big bike race (REWARD).

- *Master and Commander: The Far Side of the World*
- *Carrie*
- *Madagascar*
- *Mad Hot Ballroom*
- *Speed*
- *The Sisterhood of the Traveling Pants*
- *A League of Their Own*
- *Pirates of the Caribbean*
- *A Walk in the Clouds*
- *Antz*
- *Freaky Friday*
- *Clueless*
- *10 Things I Hate About You*
- *Ferris Bueller's Day Off*

BRAINSTORMERS

1. Look in today's newspaper and find three real-life stories which respectively demonstrate themes of reward, revenge and escape. For example, sports stories relate to the reward of excelling in competition and/or making a surprise comeback.

2. Pick an event that happened to you recently. How would you tell this story if reward was the main objective? How about revenge? How would you incorporate escape? Which of these approaches do you feel would be the most effective in telling the story? Explain your answer.

3. What kind of story do you want to write? What will be the governing objective behind the main characters' actions? To what degree will the quest be successful (e.g., will true love be found, will justice be served, will danger be dodged)?

AIMING FOR HIGH CONCEPT

In the previous chapter, you learned that conflicts are driven by reward, revenge or escape. For a stand-out script, however, a story needs to deliver more than just *a girl wins a spelling bee, a miner avenges his brother's death, or a musician tunnels his way out of a concentration camp*. While each of these can potentially be spun into a good read, none of them break new ground. For a director to give an enthusiastic thumbs-up and for moviegoers to enthusiastically part with their money for a ticket, you need to give them something fresh. What you need to give them is material that is deemed "high concept."

Screenwriting instructors often define "high concept" as a plot that can be distilled to a single sentence (in screen lingo, it's called a logline). Unfortunately, this leads to writers furiously trying to compress their entire premise into something that looks like: "*thisisaboutsomekidswhowanttogotocollegebutdon'thaveanymoneyandsotheydecide...*"

"High concept" is also explained as _____ meets _____, inviting readers to imagine the marriage of two existing films in order to understand the dynamics of a third (i.e., *Aladdin* meets *Die Hard*, *Clueless* meets *The Terminator*, *Elektra* meets *Forrest Gump*). Familiarity with the films compared sets up an easy framework of expectation.

The true test of "high concept" is one that either pairs two unlikely elements (e.g., opposite personalities sharing the same space/a fish-out-of-water hero thrust into a contrary environment) or a reversal of what we think will be traditional fare (e.g., a kidnap scheme goes awry when the ransom money is put up as bounty on the kidnappers). Whether you explain the uniqueness of your plot in one intriguing sentence or use a comparison, a "high concept" premise is one that elicits a "Wow!" without having even read the script.

LOOK & LEARN

During World War II, the Japanese excelled at deciphering military codes. There was one encryption, however, which totally stymied them and which gave U.S. troops in the Pacific an advantage. It was the unwritten language of the Navajo and was used by Native American soldiers (dubbed "windtalkers") to communicate strategic information in battle. Each of the windtalkers was assigned the equivalent of a bodyguard, so valuable was the service they were providing to the war effort. There was just one catch the Navajo weren't filled in on; the soldiers assigned to them were more committed to protecting the code than protecting the native speaker. If capture by the enemy seemed imminent, the orders were to kill them. Hooked already? *Windtalkers* is worth a look.

BRAINSTORMERS

1. Earlier in this section, three storylines were presented: (1) a girl wins a spelling bee; (2) a miner avenges his brother's death; and (3) a musician tunnels his way out of a concentration camp. Pick one of these storylines and, in a 100-word essay, explain how you would pitch it as a "high concept" movie.

2. If you were to describe the plot of the film you want to write as _____ meets _____, how would you fill in the blanks? Share this description with ten people who are unfamiliar with what you're working on. How many of them react by saying this is a movie they'd like to see?

3. Have you ever been completely surprised by the outcome of something you thought was a foregone conclusion? What was the event and how could you use it to develop a "high concept" script?

CATCHY LOGLINES

It's Friday night, your friends are all busy, and you decide to make a batch of popcorn and see what's on television. Rather than aimlessly channel-surf, you dig out last Sunday's TV section from the newspaper or hop online at *www.tvguide.com*. Among the listings you find:

- The cast members of a sci-fi series are mistaken for the real thing by aliens in desperate need of intergalactic protection.
- A mentally challenged man fights to maintain custody of his seven-year-old daughter.
- An actor is recruited to impersonate a newly deceased South American dictator.
- An island theme park featuring cloned dinosaurs becomes a place of terror when a security system malfunction sets them all loose.

What do these four mini-summations have in common? Not only are each of them short but they entice us with situations that invite major obstacles and impending crisis:

- What will happen when the aliens discover their heroes are fake?
- Will the father lose his little girl in court?
- How long can the impersonator fool a rebellious public?
- Can the humans escape their prehistoric predators?

This is the crux of a catchy logline — a tease that presents us with an intriguing question that can only be answered by watching the film itself. In the business of screenwriting, a great logline is what compels a reader to request a synopsis which, if also well written, then leads to a request for the full script. A logline is from one to three sentences long and always written in the present tense. One of the easiest ways to learn to write a solid logline is to write it first as a question. Example: "What happens when a child has a higher IQ than her mentally challenged father?" This will keep you from the first-timer's habit of trying to compress your entire plot (including its outcome) into one tell-all sentence.

A logline is only the bait that lures them close enough to your boat to catch.

LOOK & LEARN

The next time you go to movies at the mall, stroll around and check out the lobby posters of upcoming features. These will often contain a short tag that tweaks our curiosity to come back when a particular film opens. Examples:

- "Hell Wants Him. Heaven Won't Take Him. Earth Needs Him." (*Constantine*)
- "Repair for Adventure!" (*Robots*)
- "The truth needs no translation." (*The Interpreter*)
- "They don't want you to know what you are." (*The Island*)

If you're looking for more inspiration from movie posters, you'll want to bookmark *www.oscar.com/legacy/bestpicture/index.html*. This site displays the artwork of every Oscar-winning film since 1928. While some of the promos here are better written than others, this will give you a sense of the set-ups and buzz words that studios use to — well, create a buzz.

BRAINSTORMERS

1. Loglines often hint at who the main character is. Write three separate loglines for three new versions of *Casablanca* in which, respectively, Victor Lazlo, Captain Renault and Sam the piano player are each the leads.

2. Come up with ten different loglines for the film you want to write. Present these in ballot form to individuals who are not already familiar with your plot and ask them to pick the one that would most compel them to see your movie.

3. If you were going to use any event in your life as the plot of a film, what would your logline be? Remember to limit your answer to no more than three sentences and write it in the present tense. Example: Kenny's worst teacher is about to become his parents' summer houseguest.

SYNOPSES SHOULDN'T READ LIKE BOOK REPORTS

A friend of mine is always showing me her third grader's writing efforts. The latest of these is a book report that reads something like:

> This is a story about Janey. Her brother puts a fat frog named Earl in her dresser drawer. What happens when Janey opens it? Read this book and you will find out.

Yes, well, as riveting a premise as that is, it wouldn't get through the door as a film synopsis. Why? Because it's withholding pertinent information from us, specifically, the ending. Unfortunately, the instruction that many of us received under the direction of well-meaning elementary school teachers — "create suspense!" — is the wrong approach when it comes to enticing a reader to request a copy of your screenplay. A studio reader wants the proof that you know how to *finish* a story as smartly as you know how to start one. Hinting that you'll only divulge the outcome if they read your whole project will only get you one thing: absolutely nothing.

A synopsis is your script's initial "Ta-da!" calling card. It can be anywhere from one paragraph to three and follows the classic story structure of a catchy set-up, escalating complications and a satisfying resolution. The secondary purpose of a synopsis is to demonstrate that you know how to be brief. A summary that meanders all over the place is a sure tip-off that the script itself lacks focus, cohesion and merit.

Many writers fret, of course, that if they give away all their surprises in the synopsis, the reader then has no reason to read the script. Not true. Studio readers *need* to know those secrets in order to judge whether a project has any substance. Their subsequent request to read the script itself is to affirm that you can deliver on your promises.

LOOK & LEARN

The test of a great synopsis is twofold: (1) Can it be understood on the first read and (2) could the reader turn round and successfully pitch it someone else without the encumbrance of too many pesky details? Internet Movie Database (*www.imdb.com*) does a nice job of creating a hook for each of its listings, as does *www.netflix.com* in attracting customers to rent its various flicks. The only thing missing from either forum is the denouement, the one thing that *can't* be omitted from a formal studio or contest submission. Interestingly, there's a large segment of the population who want to know how a movie is going to turn out before they pay money to go see it. (These people are zealously hooked on *www.themoviespoiler.com* and also like to read the last chapters of novels first to ensure they won't be disappointed.) Pretend these people are producers or agents and tailor your synopsis to satisfy their impatience.

BRAINSTORMERS

1. Go to *www.themoviespoiler.com* and select any current movie or spoiler from the archives. After you have read the complete summary for the film you choose, write a three-paragraph start-to-finish synopsis.

2. How many words were in the three paragraph synopsis you just created? Divide that word count in half and write a *second* synopsis without sacrificing any of the core elements necessary to sell the premise and resolution of the script.

3. You have decided to enter your film short in a script competition. The rules state that you must submit a synopsis not to exceed 75 words in length. How would you meet this challenge and satisfy the requirement of classic three-act structure?

LOCATION, LOCATION, LOCATION

Your lead character — we'll call him Thatcher — has summoned the courage to approach his stunning and smart classmate Linda and pop an important question. Specifically, will she let him copy her algebra homework so Mr. Berna won't give him an "F" and get him kicked off the baseball team. In setting this scene, should Thatcher ask her (1) in the school corridor between classes; (2) over lunch at her favorite café; (3) while strolling through a dark cemetery; or (4) during a ride together on the subway.

Before you answer, here are several issues to consider: (1) is privacy important for this conversation; (2) how much time will Thatcher need to make a persuasive pitch; and (3) what kind of ambiance is most conducive to a positive response from Linda.

Where you set the action of your story is as critical as the content of each scene in it, especially in film shorts where you don't have the luxury of limitless locales. Having too many settings in a short is not only costly but also confusing to viewers in that they end up spending too little time in any one place to form any attachment. In addition, unless the identity of the environment will later be revealed as a *Twilight Zone*–style twist, it should be clear to viewers from the outset via establishing shots (e.g., a shack in the desert), costumes, cars, props and signage ("Bienvenido a México") what the locale is. Title cards are permissible as well and are often employed if some sort of "ticking clock" countdown is involved (e.g., "Emily's Dorm Room – 3 a.m.").

The genre, too, impacts a writer's choice of locations. For instance, a comedy works best in a frenetic environment, a burgeoning romance needs a set devoid of distractions, and a thriller best escalates the tension in places that are dark and isolated.

LOOK & LEARN

TV sitcoms and family programs are a good source of study for locations because they typically use one to three stock sets for every episode. These backdrops, thus, become comfortable to viewers and subliminally convey details about the fictional people who live there. For example, what do the following settings reveal about the finances, social status, upbringing, hobbies, and creature comforts (nostalgia) of the person(s) listed:

- Monica's apartment (*Friends*)
- The Camden house (*7th Heaven*)
- Dharma and Greg's living room (*Dharma and Greg*)
- Will's apartment (*Will and Grace*)
- Marie and Frank's kitchen (*Everybody Loves Raymond*)
- Eric's basement (*That 70's Show*)
- Jerry's kitchen (*Seinfeld*)
- Veronica's office (*Veronica Mars*)
- Sydney's apartment (*Alias*)

BRAINSTORMERS

1. On the previous page, you were given a choice of four locations in which Thatcher can ask his question. Pick the one that most appeals to you and, in a 100-word essay, write a summary of how this scene would play out (including Linda's answer).

2. What room are you sitting in at this very moment? Your assignment is to come up with a five-minute skit that would best fit the social/economic/personal background, size, décor and lighting of this environment.

3. Describe the film location(s) you plan to use in the short you want to write. In a 100-word essay, explain your rationale in choosing them, as well as how your choices are consistent with your selected genre and reflect something about the personalities of the characters in your script.

MASTER SCENES

During the course of a day, your footsteps will take you to a number of different locations — your bedroom, the kitchen, a bus, the school cafeteria, the gym. In each of these venues, dialogue is exchanged with whoever else happens to be there — your kid sister, the cafeteria lady with the hairnet, a fellow player on the basketball team. Once the interaction is complete, you — the star of your day — move on to the next scene. In film, each of these different venues are called "master scenes." What this means is that everything that happens within a single setting occurs under a left margin ("slug line") header such as INT. – KITCHEN, EXT. – STREET, INT. – STUDY HALL, etc. It is understood by the reader that all action will continue to transpire in this same master scene until the next slug line header reveals that the action has now shifted to a new locale.

In addition to establishing the location and whether it's indoors or outdoors, the master scene also identifies whether it's DAY or NIGHT. Further distinction can be made with notations such as EXT. – CABIN – EARLY MORNING, INT. – CASEY'S DORM ROOM – LATE AFTERNOON, etc. Two lines below the master scene is a very brief, single-spaced description of who is in this scene and what they're doing.

Example:
INT. – CASEY'S DORM ROOM – LATE AFTERNOON

College co-ed CASEY COLLINS is watching *Oprah*, noshing on pizza and doing homework. Her roommate, DARCY SMITH, stumbles in with bags of groceries.

Although you may see numbered master scenes in some of the scripts you download for study, be aware that such numbers are added by the director, not the writer, as a way to establish an efficient shooting schedule once the film goes into production.

LOOK & LEARN

The opening credits of the sci-fi thriller *The Butterfly Effect* set forth the premise that any action, no matter how seemingly inconsequential, can impact humanity on a global scale. In an attempt to decipher his ongoing blackouts and repressed memory, protagonist Ashton Kutcher travels back and forth through time, unleashing bigger problems with each attempt to "fix" them. This not only equates to a lot of different locales but also time and space continuums. For an intriguing read, download the script for free at "Screenplays For You," a website located at *http://sfy.ru*. As you read it, circle all of the master scenes in red. This exercise will not only familiarize you with correct formatting but demonstrate the importance of keeping the pace of a feature film moving by not lingering in any given scene for too long.

BRAINSTORMERS

1. In a film short, master scenes are held to a minimum to keep down expenses and keep the audience focused on a handful (or less) of characters dealing with one specific problem. For the film you want to write, list in chronological order each master scene location, time of day and — very briefly — what happens. Explain why each scene is crucial to the plot.

2. In 1865, Robert E. Lee surrendered to Ulysses S. Grant at Appomattox Court House, bringing an end to the Civil War. If you were limited to only three master scenes for a twenty-minute documentary short on this event, what would they be and why?

3. What did you do on your last birthday? To the best of your memory, compose a master scene chronology in proper format.

HOW TO BE MULTIPLE PLACES AT ONCE

In the previous chapter, you learned how master scenes comprise the framework of your story, moving the reader from one setting to the next. What happens, however, when you want to show two scenes happening simultaneously? If, for instance, your lead characters are talking on the phone and are in different parts of the city, it would eat up lots of line space to keep repeating the respective master scene descriptions as they volley their dialogue back and forth. This is where you would use what's called an "intercut."

To start an intercut, you set up the first master scene normally (e.g., INT. – MARY'S KITCHEN – NIGHT. Mary dials a number.) Set up the second scene normally, too (e.g., INT. – BILL'S OFFICE – NIGHT. Bill grabs his ringing cell phone). At the left slug line immediately below, type: INTERCUT PHONE SEQUENCE. The dialogue between Mary and Bill is then written out like a regular scene. When the conversation ends, type: END INTERCUT PHONE SEQUENCE. This returns the script to a single setting. The director decides how to divvy up actual screen time for the actors.

Intercuts are also used for short and simultaneous action segments. For instance, the first master scene could be a ballroom where elegantly dressed guests are dancing. The second scene is upstairs where a thief is burglarizing the safe. The intercut flips quickly between what the guests are doing and the progress of the intruder. The one-sentence slug-line descriptions are single-spaced with a line space between the concurrent scenes.

Example:
WAITERS circulate with trays of champagne.

A tray of diamonds is removed from the safe.

An OLDER COUPLE begins to waltz.

LOOK & LEARN

Cellular is a modern-day thriller in which a young man unwittingly becomes involved in a kidnapped woman's ordeal when her desperate attempts to resurrect a smashed phone result in dialing his cell phone number. Download the script at *www.scriptcrawler.com* for a good study example of how intercuts are used in phone conversations and action sequences. In addition to intercuts, you'll notice that the screenwriter also uses voice overs where the female character is heard but not seen on camera. Contrast this to the original screenplay for *Phone Booth*, in which the action is written in single master scenes and the characters on the phone are written as VOICE, MAVIS' VOICE, etc.

BRAINSTORMERS

1. Your assignment is to write a two-page intercut phone scene. Character 1 is in an office. Character 2 is in a quirky "tourist trap" in a distant city. How quirky? Go to the following link on your computer: *http://cityguide.aol.com/roadtrip/main.adp*. This will deliver you to a wacky list of American landmarks and weird roadside attractions. Pick a locale for Character 2 to be calling from and let the dialogue begin!

2. Write a half-page intercut action scene in which a teen's parents are en route home from an evening party and their teen is furiously cleaning up evidence of a party she's had herself.

3. Write a one-page intercut phone scene between a zealous telemarketer and a person whose ears are plugged up from a bad cold.

CONFLICT IS A COLLISION COURSE OF MULTIPLE LAYERS

Taking your hero from the start to finish of his/her quest should never look like an easy journey. If a story unfolds in which the path has no speed-bumps, worthy adversaries or past scars that have infused the protagonist's psyche with self-doubt, why would the production be worth watching? In order for your characters' collision with destiny to be as credible as it is compelling, the trick is to show that what they *want* isn't always commensurate with what they still need to *learn*. In order to accomplish this, the conflict has to embrace more than just one layer.

Film history is full of star-crossed romances, mistaken identities and cunning one-upmanship in which players seek to take advantage of one another's confidence or ignorance. What makes these plots entertaining are the layers of complication stemming from the presence of two objectives that may or may not be compatible. This co-existence is represented in "A" line and "B" line conflicts.

The primary goal (winning the big race, saving the world, falling in love, etc.) is the "A" line. For instance, Shakespeare's *Romeo and Juliet* want to get married in spite of their respective parents' objections. The secondary, "B" line goal is their desire to keep both families happy. Are we looking at a win/win outcome here? Not likely. If it were as simple as the Montagues and the Capulets sitting down together and being told by their offspring that the marriage would proceed with or without their blessing, it would make for a much shorter story. Instead, the forbidden romance forces the enlistment of confederates to keep their trysts secret, a condition that fuels an already ugly equation and results in the lovers' tragic demise. Score: no win/no win.

LOOK & LEARN

Sometimes the "A" and "B" lines are harder to pick out.

In *Death of a Salesman*, Willie Loman's "A" list expectation is that his decades of loyalty to his employer will finally result in an in-town job. The story's "B' thread, however, is about ageism and the employer's objective to phase out older workers in favor of younger ones. Accordingly, Loman's wishes run counter to the bigger picture of society's indifference toward his welfare and that of his family. Score: no win/win.

The flip side of age — being too young — is at issue in *The Member of the Wedding*. Gawky tween Frankie's primary "A" quest is for the world — or at least her family — to pay more attention to her. In this story, the parallel "B" track is her inevitable transition to young womanhood, a segue that Frankie herself is unaware of until it actually happens, thus fulfilling her need for validation. Score: win/win.

BRAINSTORMERS

1. Kelly thinks her family's new swimming pool will make her really popular with the "in" crowd at her school. She is mortified when her mom invites a geeky cousin to spend the entire summer. What are the "A" and "B" line objectives for (1) Kelly; (2) her mom; and (3) the cousin? Which ones are compatible? Which ones are not?

2. Using this same story, how would you make the outcome (1) a win/win; (2) a no win/no win; and (3) a win for one side and a loss for the other?

3. In the film you want to write, what is the primary ("A") objective? What is the secondary ("B") thread of the conflict?

A CONFLICT IS IGNITED BY AN INCITING INCIDENT

Let's say that every day you go to the school cafeteria to eat your lunch, the best table in the room is always occupied by the same obnoxious group. They're loud, they're rude, and they're exactly the kind of edgy and dysfunctional crowd that parents of any era hope their offspring will never hook up with or want to take to the prom. Although the members of this particular group are collectively as dumb as a box of rocks, no one ever steps up to challenge their crass behavior. Nor would anyone ever think to sit down at their table; even if it were totally empty at the time, the fear of discovery by the unsavory clique that has staked it out as their own has been enough to dissuade outside occupancy. Disturbing as this is to you, however, you've determined it's not really your problem.

One day a fellow student with MS who is in a wheelchair is going past the table and accidentally bumps into it. The bad crowd decides to make an example of this person by grabbing his wheelchair and spinning him around, laughing at his panicked pleas to stop. For as many months as you've kept to yourself and tried to ignore the group's conduct, they have finally crossed the line. A conflict that you previously felt had nothing to do with you personally is now a fight that calls you to action.

In screenwriting, this event is called an "inciting incident" and it's what helps set the plot in motion. Without such an event transpiring, the characters could very likely go forever without changing their routine. Suddenly — and not unlike the proverbial straw that broke the camel's back — the status quo is disrupted in such a profound way that they are now forced to make a decision and take a stand. Such action will not only impact their own lives from that moment forward but the lives of everyone around them as well.

LOOK & LEARN

Critics have argued that *Braveheart* and *The Patriot* — both starring Mel Gibson — are basically the same plot set in different centuries and countries. In *Braveheart*, William Wallace is a pacifist Scot who doesn't join the rebellion against the English until his beloved wife, Murron, is murdered. In *The Patriot*, Benjamin Martin is a pacifist farmer who doesn't join the colonial militia against the English until his beloved son, Thomas, is murdered. With both of these films, the inciting incident is so heinous that the protagonist can no longer keep tending his flock of cows and hoping that everything will quietly go away.

Contrast this to a lighter type of character reinvention such as that found in *Legally Blonde*. In this flippy comedy, the inciting incident is Elle getting dumped by her boyfriend; without this disruption in her sheltered status quo, she would never have gone to Harvard and proven she had a brain under that perfectly coiffured blonde hair.

BRAINSTORMERS

1. What are the three most recent movies you've seen? What was the inciting incident in each one? How early did the incident occur in each story?

2. Using the brief story on the previous page about the inciting incident in the school cafeteria, describe how your intervention and involvement would change (1) your life; (2) the life of the student in the wheelchair; (3) your peers; and (4) the bad bunch.

3. What is the inciting incident in the film you want to write? How will this incident challenge your character's value system, daily routine, skill level, and relationships with others?

OBJECTIVE ACCEPTANCE AND SUBJECTIVE ENGAGEMENT

In the preceding chapter, you learned that an inciting incident is what it takes to force your characters into a dynamic course of action. What does it take, however, to stir your audience into a comparable state of excitement and commitment … and keep them there? The answer hinges on how long and how often it takes them to transition from watching a scene objectively to forming a subjective attachment to the people (or animals) who happen to be in it.

Let's say you're watching the evening news and the headline story is about a hurricane that has left hundreds of people homeless. On an objective level, no one has to tell you that disasters of this caliber are terrible; you don't have to personally *know* anyone in this human drama to accept that something tragic has occurred. Suddenly the camera zooms in on a ragged little girl hugging a mud-soaked puppy

and we are inextricably pulled into a story that only seconds before was just one entry in the 6:00 line-up. Because the tragedy now has a *face* on it, that imagery now represents our own child, our own pet, our own reminiscence of past losses. From this moment on, we have a subjective attachment; we *care* what's going to happen to her next.

Good films are often a skillful mixture of objective and subjective orientations. Those which are predominantly objective in nature (e.g., *Van Helsing*) need to contain enough subjective moments, nuances and conversations in order for the characters to reveal their personalities to us. Films which are heavy on subjective scenarios (e.g., *Freaky Friday*) need the interspersing of enough objective, action-based visuals to remind us of what's really at stake on a broader level.

LOOK & LEARN

Movies which are based on known historical events are a good example of inviting objective acceptance on the part of the audience from the outset of the story. For instance, no matter how many iterations there are on the 1912 sinking of the White Star liner, Titanic, viewers *objectively* know for a fact that well over half of the passengers and crew perished in the North Atlantic. Because history has already been written, there are no expectations of an alternative ending (e.g., a surprise rescue by a fleet of Harriers). In James Cameron's 1997 version of this tragedy, audiences are *subjectively* engaged in the drama of that April night through the interactions of two entirely fictitious characters — Jack and Rose. While they know Rose survived the icy collision with destiny because she lived to identify herself as woman in the sketch many decades later, the question that really keeps them riveted is what happened to her third-class lover.

BRAINSTORMERS

1. Identify a movie or you have seen in which the audience's relationship to the plot was predominantly objective. What devices were used to promote empathy? Did objectivity take away from the experience or decrease the film's quality?

2. Identify a movie in which the central conflict of the story was intended to be primarily subjective in nature. What devices did the film use to remind viewers of the larger, objective context?

3. You have been hired to do a 30-second commercial on the importance of insuring one's possessions against damage or loss. Explain how you would hook the audience with a subjective visual.

ACTION = REACTION

In the earlier example of the bullies in the cafeteria who were tormenting the student with MS, you saw how an inciting incident compels an otherwise passive party to step in and get involved with someone else's problem. Let's take it a step further and see how the dynamics of cause and effect influence whether a single intervention at the cafeteria will resolve the problem or kick it up a notch.

If the person who intercedes as either a mediator or champion is (1) bigger than the adversaries; (2) known to possess special skills (e.g., martial arts); or (3) related to a higher authority who can make the adversaries' lives miserable (e.g., the school principal), the bullies may see the wisdom of backing off. Contrast this to a milquetoast character whose only weapon is his quick wit; the bullies now have someone new to pick on, forcing the mediator/champion to fight back even more or figure out how to recruit reinforcements. Each

action generates a *reaction*, a causal pattern of relationships that sustains a conflict — and a plot — beyond the original, inciting incident. Whether the bullies in either scenario retaliate is contingent on their view of "winning."

Are you a chess player? Each time you make a move, your opponent is forced to make a countermove which will either protect or jeopardize the other pieces on the board. This, in turn, affects your own response and so forth. Let's apply this to screenwriting. Just as one piece can't be moved without impacting the rest, each scene in a film is a necessary set-up for the one(s) that will follow. This interconnectivity is what keeps an audience's attention and keeps the flames of excitement building instead of burning out too soon because there just wasn't enough fuel to adequately maintain it.

LOOK & LEARN

In *Dave*, the owner of a Washington D.C. temp agency is asked to be a lookalike stand-in for the currently comatose President of the United States. Rather than decline on the grounds that it's lying to the public, Dave is persuaded that he has a patriotic duty to "do the right thing." Once in office, however, he quickly discovers that (1) the First Lady hates him; (2) the Chief of Staff is a sleaze; (3) the V.P. is a decent human being; (4) government funds are being spent inappropriately; and (5) the President is corrupt. Compounding his dilemma is the fact that every action he takes to undo a plethora of White House wrongs only serves to incur more venom from the Chief of Staff. How, then, can he hope to expose the truth without destroying his own life and reputation?

BRAINSTORMERS

1. *Pay It Forward* gives us a premise of people performing random acts of kindness for strangers in the hope the recipients will reciprocate with good deeds toward *other* strangers. Has a stranger ever done something for you that had a ripple effect of causing *you* to do something nice for someone else? Explain your answer.

2. *Ragtime*, the musical and film adapted from E. L. Doctorow's novel of the same name, is a Gilded Age drama that escalates from romance to rage. What was the inciting incident which set up the chain of events leading to its tragic finale? Under what circumstances could this tragedy have been avoided?

3. In *Risky Business*, mayhem ensues when a young man's parents go out of town. Starting with the inciting incident, how many complications "fuel the fire"? As you watch the film, keep a chronological list of its cause and effect events.

TO MAKE A CONFLICT CONVINCING, THE OPPONENTS NEED TO BE EVENLY MATCHED

Let's say that you're a really good tennis player. The coach at your school has you play a game against someone who's not very good. The win is an easy one, but how good do you feel about yourself afterwards? Beating someone who's not your equal takes a lot of the fun out of it and never pushes the envelope in terms of making you play your best game and improve your personal skill level. Wouldn't you feel better about your abilities if you trounced someone who was a three-time state champion?

The same is true of movie heroes and villains. If the odds are heavily stacked in the hero's favor, the villain will never come across as a scary threat. In order to make their fictional "game" worth watching, both sides need to possess comparable resources. Comparable, however, doesn't mean they have all the *same* information,

skills, advantages, and weapons. Sometimes, in fact, a villain (such as Lex Luthor) knows something that the hero (Superman) doesn't *know* he knows about (Kryptonite).

Here are some more examples to study: In *Die Hard*, the lone character of John McClane has the element of surprise in his favor; as well organized as the terrorists are, they have no idea where he's going to pop up next! In *Back to the Future*, Marty McFly has the advantage of always knowing what's supposed to happen next. In *The Sting*, Gondorff and Hooker resort to an antiquated scam in order to cheat powerful mob boss Doyle Lonnegan. Against the backdrop of outer space (e.g., *Star Wars*), the rebel forces have smaller and/or less sophisticated spaceships but this gives them the maneuverability to run circles around the larger vessels of the enemy.

LOOK & LEARN

For each of the following films, do a two-column comparison of what assets and talents the good guys have versus what the opposing forces have:

- *Superman*
- *The Great Escape*
- *Rocky*
- *National Treasure*
- *Norma Rae*
- *The Lord of the Rings: The Fellowship of the Ring*
- *Dave*
- *The Incredibles*
- *Master and Commander: The Far Side of the World*
- *Daredevil*
- *Elektra*

BRAINSTORMERS

1. Identify three movies (excluding those listed above) in which being *smart* triumphs over being *strong*. Describe key scenes in which the lead character uses his/her wits or intelligence to defeat a physically superior enemy.

2. If you could possess any superhero power (invisibility, flying, shape-changing, etc.), what would it be? Instead of being used for good, however, this power is in the hands of a villain. Describe the traits and skills a hero would need to possess in order to trap and/or defeat this nemesis.

3. In the film you want to write, what elements are in the hero's favor to accomplish his/her goal? Likewise, what resources are available to the villain that will thwart that objective? *Helpful hint*: you may want to do a two-column comparison as you did with the list of movies under "Look & Learn." This lets you see at a glance if one side or the other is "under-powered."

WHEN "LOSING" ISN'T AN OPTION

Once upon a time when I first began acting, I used to view auditions as a matter of life and death, as in "If I don't get this part, I'll completely die." Yes, in retrospect that's very much the drama queen, isn't it? One needs to understand, however, that I belonged to a circle of friends who took our craft as actors very seriously; if you weren't performing in a play or already in rehearsal for your next one, you may as well not even be breathing. Suffice it to say, there were quite a few roles I didn't land over the course of all those years. Not once, however, did I ever melt into a pathetic puddle like the Wicked Witch whenever someone threw water on my star-struck dreams. I simply looked in the newspapers and found something else to go try out for.

The point of this anecdote is that as much as I may have *wanted* a certain part, my life was never *dependen*t on getting it. Remember this when you are defining the stakes for characters in your script: they *must* achieve their goal because the consequences of losing it are much too high. It's also important to note that the consequences for a good guy will always be more dire than anything the bad guy can bring to the table. Why? Because movie villains traditionally start out with the advantage. While greed inevitably proves their downfall, the only thing they really have to do is maintain their internal status quo. Heroes, in contrast, have neither the mindset of an aggressor nor the power base to launch an offensive. Because their status quo is under external strike, they not only have to vigorously defend themselves but engage in high risks in order to win.

Unlike aspiring actors, they can't just go find another venue to test their skills. For them, this is no audition. This is It.

LOOK & LEARN

It was Andrew Jackson to whom the saying is ascribed, "One man with courage makes a majority." Earlier, British statesman Edmund Burke voiced similar sentiment in his own declaration, "The only thing necessary for the triumph of evil is for good men to do nothing." In each of the following movies, identify what would have happened if the good characters had stood by and not taken action:

- *Norma Rae*
- *It's a Wonderful Life*
- *Braveheart*
- *Harry Potter*, et al.
- *Star Wars*, et al.
- *Dave*
- *Joan of Arc*
- *Robin Hood, Prince of Thieves*
- *The Client*
- *Silkwood*
- *Spy Game*

BRAINSTORMERS

1. Using the numbers 1 through 10 (with 1 representing the least risk and 10 representing the most), rank each of the protagonists in the above films in terms of his or her degree of risk in righting a wrong.

2. Which character in your list was #10? If you ever found yourself in the same circumstances as this person, what would you do? Explain your rationale.

3. When was the last time you took a risk in order to gain something? Was it something for yourself or for another person? What were the consequences of not taking a risk? What was the final outcome? Were you satisfied that the result was worth the time and energy you invested to bring it about?

A CONFLICT CAN'T BE RESOLVED UNTIL THE END OF THE FILM

Nothing should ever look easy for the characters in your story. The reason is that audiences *want* to see them struggle and have setbacks and to nearly give up hope. While their own lives aren't *exactly* like those of the people onscreen (trying to escape being eaten by a Neptunian Sloth Monster, for instance), they still need to feel a kinship with whomever they deem to be the plucky underdog. They themselves have known what it's like to be lonely, to be afraid, to lose a fight or to miss an opportunity. Movie endings offer not only a vicarious form of redemption (e.g., you may not have won the race yourself but you're really happy your best friend did) but also impart the optimistic message about staying true to one's convictions and values, regardless of the outcome.

Where new screenwriters often make a mistake, however, is in solving their central conflict too soon and then making the characters wander around aimlessly until the final credits. Let's say, for example, that your protagonist desperately needs $100 in order to get her car repaired so she can make it to a vocal audition. Five minutes into the story, her mother asks her why she's so upset. "If I don't make that audition," she laments, "I'll never get another chance," whereupon Mom opens her purse and hands her the full amount. Problem solved. Now while you could show her getting the car fixed, singing brilliantly at the tryouts and landing a slot with a hottie boys' band, that's not the original conflict you set forth. Because the solution came easily — and early — what reason does the audience now have to continue watching the rest of your film?

Whatever conflict drives your plot, don't take your foot off the gas until the finish line is in sight. And once you *cross* that line, there's no reason to keep the motor running.

Is it possible for Death to overstay his welcome? I'm sure there are those who would argue that if the Grim Reaper really *was* personified by Brad Pitt, he'd probably be more than welcome to hang around the house indefinitely. In the 1989 film *Meet Joe Black*, Anthony Hopkins plays a millionaire who strikes a bargain to keep his demise in limbo for as long as he can keep his unbidden guest from the Hereafter entertained. The fact this movie clocks in at over two-and-a-half hours is an indicator that the inevitable ending — and the audience's patience — was drawn out well past the recommended expiration date.

Another film that didn't know when to say goodbye was the Jack Nicholson/Diane Keaton comedy *Something's Gotta Give*. In this story, a female writer is torn between romance with a man who's her own age versus a doctor who's considerably younger. Since the central question (whether "love after fifty" is still possible) had already been answered to her satisfaction, the drawn-out ending served no useful purpose in reinforcing either the quest for — or existence of — options for companionship.

1. At what point would you have ended *Meet Joe Black*? Explain your answer.

2. At what point would you have ended *Something's Gotta Give*? Explain your answer.

3. In the film you want to write, what is your main character's conflict? Identify three "easy" ways his/her problem can be instantly solved (e.g., winning the lottery). For each of these quick fixes, identify an obstacle that cancels it out (e.g., a glitch in the lottery system invalidates all of that evening's winning numbers). Which one of these obstacles will be the most formidable to overcome?

SURPRISE IS ON YOUR SIDE

Every Christmas, my father always used to ask my mother what he'd bought her. When I was a kid, I thought it was a joke. When I got older, I discovered he really had no clue. She'd simply go to Saks or Neiman Marcus, buy what she wanted, wrap it up and "act" surprised when she opened it. What a sad way to live, I thought. And what a sad way to write movies where audiences always know what's inside the box you're giving them because you've been as obvious about it as my mother buying presents for herself.

By the end of Act 1, your viewers will start making guesses about a plot's outcome. That's why you have Act 2 to introduce table-turning reversals to make them question whether their guesswork is plausible. The second act of romances, for instance, usually involves irreconcilable differences and an ugly break-up. The second act of crime stories typically calls for the prime suspect to suddenly become a victim. The second act of historically based plots such as *Titanic* introduces a crisis that will reveal the impacted characters' true natures. In Act 2, what was a foregone conclusion is now no longer something they can bank on. Act 3 — ta-da! — reveals all the cards you've had up your sleeve.

A surprise is something we don't see coming. In a successful film, an audience won't see a surprise coming if there are enough other elements like great dialogue, great characters, and great visuals to distract them from your story's true destination. To return to the gift-giving analogy, this is like putting a pair of earrings in a tiny box but hiding it in a carton full of noisy, uncooked rice. A recipient will be so preoccupied trying to envision what sort of object fits the dimensions of the container and makes that rattling noise, it never occurs to them that the box itself is only an illusion.

LOOK & LEARN

In 1927, Lon Chaney and a young ingénue named Joan Crawford appeared in a quirky silent flick called *The Unknown*. Chaney plays an armless circus performer secretly in love with his assistant, Anon, daughter of the gypsy king. But wait! The circus strong man, Malabar, loves her, too. Anon thinks he's just a big stupid brute, not kind and sensitive like her limb-challenged Alfonzo. But wait! One night the gypsy king attacks Alfonzo. Malabar saves his life. In repayment, Alfonzo gives him bad advice on how to pursue Anon, advice Alfonzo secretly knows will scare her. But wait! Alfonzo has even more up his sleeves; specifically, a perfectly good pair of arms. Why this duplicity? To conceal his identity as a wanted man! His best pal, Cojo the dwarf, warns him that Anon will hate him if she learns his deformity is a fraud. But wait! Alfonzo decides to pay a surgeon to *amputate* his arms so that — well, you get the picture.

BRAINSTORMERS

1. Identify three films with endings that totally blew you away. What devices were employed by the writer and/or the producer to distract you from figuring it out prematurely?

2. You have been selected to write a new screenplay based on the story of Robinson Crusoe. In the vein of such films as *The Crying Game*, *The Sixth Sense*, or *Planet of the Apes*, describe the kind of surprises you would incorporate in your plot that would make viewers say "Wow!"

3. In real life, what was the best trick you ever pulled on someone? In a 100-word essay, explain why the trick worked (e.g., the subject's gullibility, the use of accomplices, etc.). How could this be applied to successfully fooling an audience?

CONFLICT GROWS OUT OF CHARACTER

As you're sitting in class, take a brief glance around the room. How many people would you count as really good friends? How many of them conjure exactly the opposite feelings? How many of them (including your teacher) are such an enigma that — even after an entire semester — you still haven't figured out what makes them tick?

Let's say you're going to be broken into different teams and assigned to come up with an idea for the end-of-year school party. If this is something you and your best friends have already been talking about and looking forward to, you're probably all on the same page. Sit on a committee together? No prob. But what if the team you're assigned to is made up of the kids you either (1) don't like or (2) don't know? Even though the destination itself (the party) will be a lot of fun, each person in your group will bring radically different ideas on the "right" way to plan it.

In a movie, the stakes are much higher. Conflict becomes the intersection where the participants' respective intentions, beliefs, and past experiences all crash into each other. As we've seen in previous chapters, a story without conflict is a story about nothing. Likewise, conflict itself can't *emerge* from nothing; it needs to be fueled by the clash of wills that occurs whenever people who feel they have nothing in common are forced to share the same space. Bringing these dissimilar personalities together is what ignites the conflict that will then drive the plot.

Unlike a classroom where you only have to spend a short time each day with people not of your choosing, your script is a figurative "locked room" in which the characters must either learn to co-exist with their differences or to disable the opposition.

LOOK & LEARN

In *Lethal Weapon*, we have the characters of Roger Murtaugh and Martin Riggs. Murtaugh (Danny Glover) is the older, by-the-book detective and family man who's just counting the days to his retirement. Riggs (Mel Gibson) is a loose cannon — an unorthodox, manic detective with a death wish. Unlike the happily married Murtaugh, Riggs is a widower who's not afraid to take dangerous risks because, quite frankly, life has held no meaning for him since the death of his wife.

When Murtaugh and Riggs are assigned to work together, their partnership is that "locked room" we just talked about. Neither one can simply say "no" and walk out because this is what they both do for a living. Compounding this uncomfortable liaison is the fact that they also have a crime they have to solve. Murtaugh has his views on how this should be approached; Riggs holds an opposite opinion. Which one is "right"?

BRAINSTORMERS

1. Write about a situation at school or home in which the personalities of you and someone else were different enough to create an ugly conflict.

2. Identify a movie (other than *Lethal Weapon*) in which two lead characters with incompatible personalities and beliefs are forced to solve a problem together for the common good. Identify a second movie where the lead characters are adversaries and have opposite expectations of the conflict's outcome.

3. In your own story, list three character traits of your hero and three traits of your villain. Which combination of traits will most likely ignite a conflict? (Example: your hero is a pacifist; your villain likes to incite rebellions.)

CHARACTER GROWS OUT OF CONFLICT

Human beings are a work in progress. Whatever you wanted to grow up to be when you were four years old is probably quite a bit different than your career aspirations at age fourteen. The degree of conflict introduced to your life has also increased as you've gotten smarter and assumed more responsibility for your actions. Specifically, instead of worrying that you're not going to get another cookie that could spoil your dinner, your anxieties have shifted to whether you should tell someone that your best friend is starving herself to death in order to be as thin as a model.

Both the volume and complexity of problems that are now being thrown your way as a young adult will force you into deciding whether you want to confront them directly, deny their existence, or start frantically making a mad dash for the nearest exit. The bad news is that they're going to keep coming for the rest of your life. The good news, however, is that you'll hone your skills in learning how to effectively deal with them.

In a movie, the characters are forced to confront their fears, flaws and value systems when presented with a problem that they've never faced before. Whether it's a rampaging monster that comes into town or a loved one who's moving out of the picture, the lead character is called upon to make some adjustments to their thinking. If this conflict had *not* been introduced, things would have pretty much stayed status quo.

As you'll see in the next chapter, this evolution is called the "character arc." Whoever this person was at the outset — or whatever he or she believed in — will be challenged as a result of the conflict, a condition which will foment the seeds that will challenge this character to expand beyond previous limitations by the final scene.

LOOK & LEARN

In *The Fugitive*, Dr. Richard Kimble is an upstanding citizen, a respected surgeon, and a devoted husband. If we looked into his profile, he probably never even had so much as a parking ticket or overdue library book. That squeaky clean image, however, is shattered when he's charged with the murder of his wife and sentenced to death. When the prison bus carrying him to his fate collides with a train, the previously law-abiding Kimble realizes the only way to escape execution is to go on the run and try to find the murderer himself. This forces him to tap abilities and resources he would not have otherwise used and to become a stronger individual in the process.

BRAINSTORMERS

1. What are you the most afraid of? What type of emergency would have to occur in order for you to face this fear and, accordingly, overcome it? (Example: You have always been afraid of the water. Your baby sister falls into the backyard pool and there is no one else around to help rescue her.)

2. Write about a social situation (e.g., asking someone for a date) where you were really nervous. How did you overcome this fear … or is it still hanging out there and holding you back?

3. What is the hero of your film afraid of? How did this particular fear come about? What kind of conflict is necessary for the hero to face his or her fears and/or weaknesses? *Hint*: The consequences of not acting at all need to be greater than the onus of having this fear/flaw itself. Example: In *The Fugitive*, the wrongfully accused Kimble faces a death sentence unless he acts to find the real killer.

CHARACTER AND CONFLICT COMPRISE THE HERO'S JOURNEY

One of the phrases you'll often hear used in screenwriting is "the hero's journey." What this refers to is the path that a protagonist follows — oftentimes reluctantly — in order to become worthy of our praise as spectators and subsequently provide himself with the validation that he's a good person. The issue of redemption figures prominently in this awareness, giving us characters who have allowed their flaws — whether real or imagined — to define their entire value to humanity.

This is based on the classical mythical structure developed by Joseph Campbell, an American writer whose studies of folklore and archetypes showed that heroes are commonly thrust into circumstances that force them to confront demons from their past and/or inhibitions that have prevented them from moving forward in their lives. Interestingly, however, it's not the actual success or failure of the challenge itself that wins us over; it's the struggle — the journey — which inspires us.

This journey is especially poignant in coming-of-age stories, allowing us to glimpse the building blocks of a foundation that will later shape and influence a teen or tween's life. The following examples provide good material for study and comparison:

- *Saint Ralph* — a young boy equates winning the Boston Marathon to causing a miracle that will help his cancer-ridden mother.
- *Drumline* — a Harlem drummer is recruited for a school band competition.
- *Save the Last Dance* — an aspiring teen ballerina feels responsible for her mother's death.
- *Little Women* — the March sisters struggle to keep their family and their community together during the Civil War.
- *The Wonder Years* (TV series) — growing up in the confusion of the 1960s, as seen through the eyes of Kevin Arnold.
- *She's All That* — a high school hottie takes a page from *Pygmalion*.
- *Valiant* — a young wood pigeon aspires to join the Royal Air Force Homing Pigeon Service during World War II.

LOOK & LEARN

Frank Capra's Christmas classic, *It's a Wonderful Life*, examines the concept of the hero's journey in reverse fashion. Specifically, we first meet protagonist George Bailey at a bridge on a snowy night. Everything in his small-town world has gone from bad to worse and he sees no solution but to escape his problems by jumping into the freezing waters below and ending it all. His act of desperation, however, is interrupted by the arrival of a bumbling angel who is on a vision quest of his own — to prove that every life has value and that George has accomplished far more as a human being than he has ever given himself credit for.

BRAINSTORMERS

1. Not every story is destined for a happy ending. Many movies that stay with us, however, are those in which the main character grew stronger as a result of *not* getting what he or she wanted. Choose any film that you feel fits this description and, in a 100-word essay, explain how the protagonist emerged as a better person.

2. What is the unrealized potential you see in someone who is close to you? What do you feel is holding this person back? What event or circumstance would it take in order for him or her to successfully move forward?

3. In the film you want to write, tell us how your hero would complete each of the following sentences:
   (1) The Fates have cursed me with _____ ;
   (2) The Fates have blessed me with _____ ;
   (3) No one would believe me if I said I was _____ ;
   (4) The thing I most regret about my past is _____ .

CROSSING THE POINT OF NO RETURN

Once upon a time I worked in an office that had me questioning whether it was some sort of payback for evil deeds I'd done in a prior life. Not only was the supervisor an incompetent micromanager but office nepotism found me sharing space with two bubblebrain co-eds who dressed like hookers, ate smelly burritos at their desks and spent an hour every morning at the water cooler recapping their dates from the previous night. That management routinely ignored these lapses in decorum made me desperate to seek classier pastures. Unfortunately, I had no immediate job prospects lined up to replace what they were paying me to be miserable. "You're a writer," my friend Celeste said. "Why don't you just quit and write full-time?" I was dubious. What if I failed? "What if you never try?" she countered, reminding me of the "leap of faith from the lion's mouth" in the third Indiana Jones film. As long as I didn't look down, she quipped, I'd be okay.

The next day, with resignation letter in hand and feeling like a bungee jumper sans bungee, I walked down the hall to the vice president's office. At any point before I reached the threshold, I knew I could turn back. I didn't. I entered his office, handed him the envelope, smiled and walked out. From that day forward, I've been a full time writer, the dream I always wanted but might not have had without that first, perilous step.

The journey your screenplay hero takes will call for a leap of faith as well. Once he or she crosses the point of no return, there are no do-overs, no rewinds, no time-warps that can return them to life as they once knew it. No matter how safe or convenient the harbor one originally departs from, the circumstances have to be such that it's no longer a tolerable place to be, daring your hero to take a chance on what could be the destination of a lifetime.

LOOK & LEARN

In each of the following movies, identify the protagonist's "point of no return" — the definitive moment which seals his or her commitment to seeing the conflict through to resolution.

- *A Walk in the Clouds*
- *Braveheart*
- *Dave*
- *Finding Nemo*
- *Galaxy Quest*
- *High Noon*
- *Jurassic Park*
- *Master and Commander: The Far Side of the World*
- *Ragtime*
- *Robin Hood, Prince of Thieves*
- *Sister Act*
- *The Patriot*
- *Tootsie*
- *Witness*

BRAINSTORMERS

1. Your character hits the SEND button on an email without double-checking the address. When the recipient accepts his invitation to an upcoming event, he realizes his horrible mistake. In a 100-word essay, tell us who the recipient is, what the event is, and what the dire consequences could be if he attempts to back-pedal and retract his invitation.

2. Your action/adventure hero has a 100% chance of saving nine out of ten people. If he/she attempts to save *all* ten, however, the odds drop to 50%. Assuming the tenth person is a loved one and that the hero's decision is irreversible, what will he/she resolve to do? Explain your answer in a 100-word essay.

3. In the film you want to write, what is your protagonist's point of no return? If your character does not commit to this particular course of action, what would the outcome likely be? How many others in the story will ultimately be impacted by your protagonist's decision?

A CHARACTER ARC IS A TRANSFORMATION

When a character decides to do something, the storyline becomes a testament to just how strong that commitment will be. Will the obstacles on the journey from Point A to Point B prove so overwhelming that he or she will eventually cave in and give up? Or will they instead encourage the emergence of wits and strengths that will enable the hero to succeed beyond expectations?

When a movie starts out, the hero comes into it with a set of opinions and attitudes that have been shaped by the past and the influence of others. Once the conflict is introduced and the stakes start to escalate, those opinions and attitudes become subject to re-evaluation. If a character such as Benjamin Martin in *The Patriot*, for instance, has declared that he wants no part of the Revolutionary War, how will he or she react when his own son is killed by the enemy? Can Martin continue to look away or will it be necessary to put a new definition on long-held beliefs?

A lead character's growth will resonate far more with an audience than the particulars of the conflict itself. The reason is that they recognize life isn't static and that people are constantly reinventing themselves — even subconsciously — in order to either buck the system or remain a part of it. That's why "soulless" action movies rarely work.

Even a character who *doesn't* perceptibly change — maintaining a straight path in contrast to undergoing a traditional arc — has made a statement in and of itself and is presumably even more committed to his/her agenda than was evident when the story began. Accordingly, this character serves the purpose of being a catalyst for the transformational arcs and growth of others. Example: Hannibal Lechter (*Silence of the Lambs*).

LOOK & LEARN

In *Moonstruck*, Loretta Castorini is a widow who is old beyond her years and hopes to lift the curse of her first marriage by getting engaged to Johnny Cammareri, a lackluster, indecisive man who — by her own admission — she doesn't really even love. When she meets his estranged and mercurial brother, Ronny, the flood of passions released from this relationship causes Loretta not only to rethink her own value system and attitudes toward marriage but to physically transform herself from someone listless and dowdy into someone driven and dazzling.

BRAINSTORMERS

1. Identify a movie in which the lead character radically changes his/her beliefs between the beginning of the film and the end. What events or influences caused this transformation to occur? Example: In *Monsters, Inc.*, Baby Boo teaches Sully and Mike that children aren't nearly as scary and toxic as the propaganda of Monstropolis would have everyone believe.

2. Identify a feature film in which the lead character maintains the same beliefs and objectives from start to finish. How does this steadfastness cause the other characters around him/him to alter their own perceptions from what they were at the beginning? Example: *Gandhi*.

3. What does the lead character in your story believe in? Is this a belief to which he/she will stay committed for the duration of the film? Why or why not? If not, what events or influences of other characters will cause his/her mindset to undergo a transformation?

HEROES AREN'T 100% GOOD; VILLAINS AREN'T 100% BAD

As you learned earlier, heroes and villains need to be equally matched in order to make their confrontations watchable. Further, the level of commitment each side brings to the equation will impact whether they end up staying true to their beliefs or will modify/abandon them in favor of a different view. New writers often make the mistake of creating heroes so shiny and virtuous that they practically achieve god-like stature. At the same time, they craft villains who are really mean and rotten "just because." What they don't take into account is the thin line that exists between good and evil. Save for a minor tweak of circumstances or mentors, a villain could become a champion of justice just as easily as a hero — devastated by misfortune — could turn to a dark life of crime. What makes an audience pay attention is that they see in these fictional characters the potential for good and evil that lives within themselves (e.g., *Lord of the Flies*.)

For a hero to be believable, he or she needs to have some "unfinished business" that will open the door to redemption. A character, for instance, who feels guilty about fleeing a fire in which others perished will inevitably find history repeating itself and be forced into a decision that will put past nightmares to rest. At the same time, a villain has to possess enough charisma, confidence and organizational skills not only to attract followers but to elude capture. Such are the qualities that appeal to most everyone's childhood delight of seeing just how much they can get away with in terms of bad behavior before they eventually get caught.

Who are some of Hollywood's best heroes and villains? Check out *www.afi.com* and click on the left-hand "AFI's 100 Years Series" to find out.

LOOK & LEARN

In *National Treasure*, the character of Ben Gates enlists the aid of fortune hunter Ian Howe to pursue a legendary Knights Templar treasure hidden by America's forefathers through a series of cryptic clues. When it becomes apparent Gates and Howe aren't on the same altruistic page, the latter shifts into the role of villain — a move which sets into play a competition that brings out the best of both sides' resources. How would the dynamics have been different if (1) Ben wasn't as intent on clearing his family's name and (2) Ian wasn't as greedy in wanting the treasure for himself? This movie is a great example of a hero and villain who are both likable in different ways and who aptly reflect the proverb that a person's worst enemy is someone who was once a closest friend.

BRAINSTORMERS

1. Sometimes we dislike others because they have qualities we either envy (e.g., popularity) or secretly dislike about ourselves (e.g., always wanting to be the boss). In this exercise, identify three traits you admire about the person you like the least. Explain why.

2. Sometimes we overlook flaws in those we love or feel responsible for because we don't want to upset them by mentioning it (e.g., a relative who won't quit smoking). Identify the trait you like the least in the person you care for the most. Why did this trait evolve?

3. In the script you want to write, describe what events or influences caused your hero to grow up "good" instead of "bad." Describe what events or influences caused your villain to grow up "bad" instead of "good."

SIDEKICKS, CONFIDANTES AND CONFEDERATES

Where would we be without our friends? Imagine a world where you had no one to hang out with, seek advice from, confide juicy secrets to, hitch a ride from or rely on to cheer you up whenever the universe comes crashing down. Movie heroes and villains need a circle of buds in their lives, too, although for entirely different reasons. These associates are collectively known as sidekicks, confidantes and confederates — supporting characters without whom the main players' quests would be that much more difficult. In addition to helping carry the ball, these characters are often incorporated as the means for a hero or villain to let an audience know what's going on in his or her head without having to resort to voice overs, contrived soliloquies or breaking the fourth wall.

For heroes, these characters fill the role of sounding board, pep squad and devil's advocate, providing the necessary encouragement to see the task through to completion. Villains, in contrast, already *have* all the motivation they desire; what they need is a core group of expendable hit-men flunkies who will do their jobs without question and never aspire to promotion. A hero's buddies are in the relationship for the long-term; a villain's recruits are more interested in the prize than in warm and fuzzy camaraderie. Likewise, a villain's ensemble is quick to scatter as soon their leader is killed; a hero's team is committed enough to the cause itself to keep on fighting in the name of their fallen pal.

Cohorts from either camp, of course, abide by a common code that writers need to be aware of; specifically, a sidekick's own story, dilemma, shtick, or lines of dialogue must never, ever upstage their boss. Not only do such faux pas detract from the hero's (and villain's) journey but annoy lead actors who dislike supporting players stealing their thunder.

LOOK & LEARN

In *Die Hard*, Hans Gruber (Alan Rickman) has assembled an elite team of thugs to not only hold the occupants of an L.A. high-rise hostage during a Christmas Eve party but orchestrate a theft — and escape — of enormous magnitude as well. Waging a one-man battle against Gruber and his cold-blooded confederates is New York cop John McClane (Bruce Willis), a man whose wife is one of the executives being held captive. But wait! McClane actually has an ally on the outside he hasn't even met in person yet — an African American police sergeant (Reginald Veljohnson) who intercepts McClane's call for help and is initially the only member of the LAPD who believes McClane's story that the building is under siege. The fragile trust that develops between them — and the sergeant's subsequent act of redemption at story's end — is an excellent example for applying what you have just learned about the chemistry of companions.

BRAINSTORMERS

1. In the Disney comedy *Sky High*, the offspring of superheroes are divided into two groups — those with super powers and those relegated to the role of sidekicks. If the student body at your school were similarly divided, which faction would you belong to? If you were a superhero, who would you want as *your* sidekick? If you were a sidekick, who would be the superhero you'd hang with? Explain why.

2. Who is your favorite "good guy" sidekick in the movies? What role or function does this character serve for the hero (e.g., advice, comic relief, back-up)?

3. Who is your favorite "bad guy" sidekick in the movies? What role or function does this character serve for the villain (e.g., brawn, pawn, Yes-man)?

ORDINARY CHARACTERS NEED EXTRAORDINARY SITUATIONS

What do you usually do after school or on weekends? Do you do chores? Do you do homework? Do you go to the mall? Do you hang out with friends and play games or listen to music on your iPod? Each of these activities is fairly ordinary, structured and generally leads to predictable outcomes. If you tried to write a movie in which these were the *only* things that ever happened to your characters, however, your audience would get bored pretty fast. Why? Because it's all too much like real life! (Yawn.)

While it's perfectly okay to write about ordinary people (and lots of authors use their friends and family for this exact purpose), it's *not* okay to fill every page of the script with stuff that's dull, conventional and unsurprising. To hook an audience and keep their attention, something *extraordinary* needs to occur early in the story that will force your characters to rethink their priorities, scramble to learn new skills, or cope with unexpected crises for which there was no prior dress rehearsal.

What if, for instance, you encountered a leprechaun in a box of detergent? What if an earthquake struck while you were at school and you had no way of contacting anyone you knew? What if you woke up tomorrow and discovered that you were invisible? What if a spaceship crashed in your backyard? What if your parents announced they were inviting your least favorite teacher to dinner?

What each of these hypothetical situations has in common is that the lead character — you — is suddenly confronted with something weird, dangerous, tragic, shocking or wonderful that has never happened before. What if these very things happened to your fictional hero? Where would the story go from there?

LOOK & LEARN

Computer-generated universes were still fairly new territory in 1982 when Disney's *TRON* made its debut. In this story, a computer whiz kid named Flynn discovers that the latest video game programs he invented were stolen by a villain named Dillinger, a crafty cad who covered his tracks and embedded the details of his thievery within the computer itself. To prevent Flynn from exposing his misdeeds to the world, Dillinger uses his familiarity with technology to literally break Flynn into byte-sized pieces and insert him into the computer matrix. As well-versed as the human Flynn is in all the nuances of video gamesmanship, the stakes are a lot higher when he becomes more of an "insider" than he ever imagined.

BRAINSTORMERS

1. Identify three movies in which an ordinary character's life is challenged by extraordinary events or circumstances. (Example: *The Princess Diaries*.)

2. What is the most unusual, unexpected or frightening thing that has ever happened to you? Describe your initial reaction to these circumstances. What resources were available to you in order to deal with this change in the status quo? What did you specifically learn from this experience and how would you apply this knowledge if it were ever to happen again?

3. Compose a short story in which your family wins the lottery. Describe how each family member's life (including your own) would be changed as a result of this sudden fortune. Where would you live? What kind of people would come into your new world? What kind of problems would arise that were not present prior to purchasing the winning ticket? Is a life of wealth everything you expected?

EXTRAORDINARY CHARACTERS NEED ORDINARY SITUATIONS

Have you ever felt like an outsider?

Maybe it was because you came from a different part of the world or practiced different customs than your peers. Maybe you were really brainy or had a special talent that far exceeded that of your friends and subsequently became cause for jealousy. Or maybe it was because your value system kept you from caving in to the pressures of what was considered cool or trendy. Whatever the circumstances that distinguish(ed) you from the herd, there's a certain amount of loneliness that comes with being "different." In film, this is the ongoing challenge that confronts gifted individuals who are trying to coexist with everyone else who has been deemed "normal."

As we just saw in the last chapter, an ordinary person's status quo needs to be shaken up in order to hook an audience's interest and make them wonder what they would do in the same situation.

Likewise, an audience will feel a kinship with *extraordinary* individuals who are either trying to assimilate into an ordinary group, maintain a healthy distance from it, or encourage the members of the group to reinvent themselves in the image and mindset of the nonconformist gatecrasher.

While superheroes, extraterrestrials and artistic virtuosos easily spring to mind as fitting the definition of "extraordinary," the same measure applies to screen characters such as *Forrest Gump* or Dustin Hoffman's *Rain Man* whose mental and/or physical limitations would seem to rule out their acceptance by the mainstream. Invariably, the lesson such characters impart is that we all have something we can learn from one another, regardless of the dissimilarities that would strive to divide us.

LOOK & LEARN

- In *Billy Elliot*, an eleven-year-old boy in an English mining town is torn between his love of — and affinity for — ballet and his family's expectation that he will not only embrace boxing as a manly sport but will eventually work in the mines like everyone else.

- In *Yentl*, an exceptionally smart Jewish girl with a thirst for learning disguises herself as a boy in order to go to the Yeshiva, a male-only school focusing on the study of the Torah.

- How hard is it to take care of an ordinary little child? A trio of extraordinary men — an architect, an actor and an artist — find out in *Three Men and a Baby*.

- There's something about Mary — *Mary Poppins*, that is. How else do you account for someone who glides through the sky with an umbrella, makes housecleaning a snap and dances with cartoon penguins?

BRAINSTORMERS

1. Identify three movies in which an extraordinary person has to function in an ordinary environment. (Example: *Bewitched*.)

2. We don't often think of Hollywood stars having to cope with mundane problems. Compose a short story in which Jack Nicholson gets a flat tire in the middle of nowhere and has no idea what he should do about it.

3. Identify someone in distant history whom you consider to be extraordinary (e.g., Nostradamus). If by a fluke of time travel he or she had to stay with you for a whole weekend, describe how you would keep your family, friends, nosy neighbors and anyone else from finding out who this person really is.

HOOKS, FORESHADOWING AND UH-OH'S

Before you throw yourself into a dynamic exercise routine, experts advise that you take some time to warm up and get your muscles prepped for what's about to happen. The same advice, however, cannot be applied to the exercise of writing dynamic screenplays. From page one, you need to hit the deck running and not stop until you're done. Why? Because neither studio readers nor audiences have the patience to slog through the first hour of a script in the hopes it will somehow heat up. If the opening scene's not a grabber, why should we hang around until FADE TO BLACK?

Think of some of the great films with eye-popping visuals, intriguing characters, daring questions or heartfelt narratives that hooked us right from the start: *Big Jake*, *Citizen Kane*, *Forrest Gump*, *Jaws*, *National Treasure*, *Raiders of the Lost Ark*, *While You Were Sleeping*. From the first frame, we're already asking, "What happens next?!"

Consider as well the skillful placement of foreshadowing in films such as *Back to the Future* where the reference to the broken clock tower later supplied the solution to Marty and Doc Brown's time-travel crisis. Introduced early (and subtly) to tease our curiosity, such elements of set-up sidestep the cliché of contrivance in the later clinches.

Also critical is the art of the Big Uh-Oh. Just when the finish line looms in sight, there's suddenly one final obstacle. The uh-oh circles back to a film's initial hooks and foreshadowing, a good example of this being *Jumanji*. Hopelessly trapped by his enemy, Alan Parrish fumbles the dice… but rolls the fortuitous combination that will finally release him and his friends from danger. What viewers have forgotten up until now, of course, is the premise that once the game is over, everything will revert to its original state.

LOOK & LEARN

Once upon a time in elementary schools far, far away, maps of the world used to display the former USSR in bright red and labeled "Russia," a blanket title synonymous (in those days) with Communism. Such views seem dated now, as does the 1990 film, *The Hunt for Red October*, in which a Soviet submarine commander may or may not be trying to defect to the United States. It's used in this chapter because it effectively illustrates the relationship of hooks, foreshadowing and uh-ohs. In this case, the hook and uh-oh relate to the presence of two Soviet submarines, not just the one. The foreshadowing references a phobia experienced by Alec Baldwin's character, a phobia which he will be required to confront before the film is over.

BRAINSTORMERS

1. Identify three films you have seen which had powerful hooks. What were they and why did they immediately grab your attention? What type of hook do you plan to use in your own film to immediately grab the audience's attention?

2. Identify three films or TV programs which contained foreshadowing. Did the information imparted *seem* like a clue at the time or was its placement not made clear to you until later on in the story? Do you plan to use foreshadowing in your own story? Explain how.

3. Identify three films in which something unexpected happened just before the end (e.g., a character you thought was dead turned out not to be). Does your own script contain an uh-oh? Is this uh-oh plausible based on the sequence of events that led up to its occurrence?

A CHARACTER SHOULD DO MORE THAN JUST TAKE UP SPACE

The more characters you have written into your screenplay, the more expensive that movie is going to be. Why? Because even if (1) they're wearing clothes they pulled out of their own closets; (2) the whole storyline unfolds in a neighbor's backyard; and (3) you're directing it yourself, a higher number of cast members will result in longer amounts of time that it will take to get all of them to learn their parts and do your bidding. You'll probably also have to feed them lunch and snacks, reimburse them for their gasoline or bus fare and, as an extra incentive to be in the film, pay them some sort of fee for their acting.

While big production companies aren't as daunted by finances as start-up filmmakers who have to max out their credit cards in order to buy camera equipment, learning from the beginning to write economically will force you to keep a tight focus on what — and *who* —

is really essential to the heart of your story. This is especially important when you're writing a short because you have less time available than in a feature to convey your idea to an audience. Each character in your project, therefore, has to perform a unique function or deliver a specific line that:

1. Advances the plot;
2. Thwarts the hero's goal;
3. Provides necessary background information; and/or
4. Contributes to the ambiance or mood of the scene.

If you've included characters in your story that don't fulfill one or more of these jobs, they probably aren't critical to the script and should be written out.

LOOK & LEARN

In *Butch Cassidy and the Sundance Kid*, there are several minor characters who appear only once during the course of the movie and yet serve to either supplement our knowledge of the three main players or to enhance our awareness of the times in which they lived (the turn of the century).

- The card player in the opening scene establishes Sundance's skill with a gun.

- The Hole-in-the-Wall gang explains the workings of Butch's home turf.

- The Large Woman creates a foil to trick Woodcock into opening the door.

- The bike salesman shows how progress will change the face of the West.

- Sheriff Bledsoe suggests foreshadowing that the days of outlaws are numbered.

- The young Bolivian stable boy whose attentiveness confirms that the two newcomers are, in fact, the notorious American bandits.

BRAINSTORMERS

1. In the movie *The Princess Bride*, there are a number of supporting roles. Using the four criteria listed on the previous page, identify three of these minor characters and explain what purpose they each have in the story. (Example: Miracle Max — played by Billy Crystal — is needed to revive the "dead" Wesley.)

2. Compose a story in which two people are being set up on a blind date. Use as few characters as you can in this plot and make sure that each one has a good reason for being there. (Example: a mutual friend who likes to play matchmaker.)

3. How many characters are in the film that you want to write? Identify why each one is important to your plot. *Hint*: The line(s) they deliver or the actions they perform could not plausibly be carried out by anyone else in the cast.

MINOR CHARACTERS DON'T NEED MAJOR INTRODUCTIONS

In the previous chapter's example of *Butch Cassidy and the Sundance Kid*, you learned how minor characters are instrumental in providing useful information about the rest of the story. You may have also noticed that — with the exception of Sheriff Bledsoe — four of the characters listed don't have names. (The Hole-in-the-Wall members *do* have names and are individually addressed as such by Butch in the movie.)

From their respective looks, actions and/or lines of dialogue, this is what we know about them:

- The card player is better skilled with cards than guns.
- The Large Woman is an outspoken grandmother who has fought whiskey and gambling and is totally fearless. Her clothes suggest affluence.
- The bike salesman is a shrewd opportunist.
- The stable boy is poor, eager to work, observant and honest.

We don't really need to learn anything more about these people because details such as where they were born, what their families are like or whether they have secret ambitions aren't relevant contributions to a plot that revolves around Butch, Sundance and Etta. While many new writers feel they have to justify every character's on-screen presence by giving him/her a name and a substantive "history," the reality is that all of these particulars not only clutter up the script but trick an audience into thinking that they're actually going to *need* this information later to understand what's going on.

Let's make an analogy to studying for an exam: Would you force yourself to memorize an entire book when the only portion of it that you knew you were going to be tested on was Chapter 3? The same applies to audiences: Don't make them memorize anything more than is absolutely necessary to follow the plot and the interactions.

LOOK & LEARN

In the 1990 film *Ghost*, Patrick Swayze portrays a young investment counselor who gets killed during a mugging and attempts to communicate crucial details about his death to his girlfriend Molly from beyond the grave. There are a number of minor characters throughout this movie who put in a one-shot appearance. As you watch it, keep a running list of these players (both the human ones and the ghostly apparitions) and identify (1) whether or not they have actual names; (2) what their purpose is for being in the story; and (3) how much background information has been provided about them by the screenwriter.

BRAINSTORMERS

1. Which one of the nameless characters in *Ghost* would you like to have known more about? Although they were not "star quality" in this film, your assignment is to write a one-page biography on this person (name, education, family, lifestyle, hobbies, etc.) and come up with a plot in which he or she would be the central figure. (Example: One of the furniture movers wins the New York lottery and can finally afford a spiffy loft like Sam and Molly's.)

2. How would your nameless character register with your best friend? Write a short letter in which your best friend is telling you about a first encounter with this person. Would he or she be impressed, bored, confused, annoyed, intrigued, impatient, indifferent, frightened or amused?

3. Compose biographies for each of the characters in the film that you want to write. Which details about their backgrounds are truly crucial to the plot? Which ones can be omitted? Provide justification for your answers.

DESIGNER GENES

When I was in high school, a lot of summer afternoons were spent by the pool reading Gothic romances and multi-generational sagas about plucky governesses overcoming adversity and going to live in well-appointed manor houses. The author of one such series was a former interior designer whose knowledge of fabrics, accessories, fixtures and furnishings manifested in chapters dominated by lengthy descriptions of who wore what, the type of chair he or she sat in, and whether the plates upon which dinner was served were Lenox, Royal Daulton or Wedgwood. Reading so many details at a time, of course, usually forced me to go back and refresh my memory on who, exactly, I'd been reading about. Try this in a screenplay and it's a sure bet a reader's attention span won't make it past page two.

As you learned in the prior chapter, a lot of details are expendable, especially if they don't advance our understanding of the players, their motivations, or the plot itself. Does it matter, for instance, that your heroine is wearing a blue plaid dress instead of a green striped one? Is it crucial your hero possess a pair of Nikes instead of Adidas? Will someone driving a 1990 Geo Tracker solve the mystery faster than if it were a 1991 Geo Storm? Does the entry to the villain's house have to be flanked by Doric columns or could Corinthian suffice? Does the banker *have* to be forty-seven, Latvian and balding?

The more generic your descriptions, the faster and more easily your script can be read. Insider secret: the more easily a script can be read, the greater the chances of it advancing up the decision-making ladder. Still can't let go of all those details? You can always try your hand at a novel or short story and use them there.

LOOK & LEARN

Go to *www.scriptcrawler.com* or any of the other free screenplay web-sites and download each of the following scripts for review. As you read them, make note of how much or how little attention is paid to details regarding the characters' clothing, possessions and physical surroundings.

- *Dave*
- *Being There*
- *Highlander 3*
- *Men in Black*
- *Pleasantville*
- *War of the Worlds*
- *Braveheart*
- *Legally Blonde*
- *Dumb and Dumber*
- *Scream 2*

It's just as important, of course, not to go *too* light on descriptions in your own scripts. If you write, for instance, "BOB enters the room," we have no idea if Bob is five or fifty, well dressed or shabby, etc.

BRAINSTORMERS

1. Based on your reading of the scripts listed above, what generalizations can you make regarding the necessity of incorporating detailed descriptions versus leaving it entirely to the discretion of the director?

2. Download the script of a film that you know nothing about (including who starred in it). As you read it, jot down notes regarding your first impressions of the characters' looks, clothing and environment. The second step is to rent the movie and see how closely your impressions match the finished product. How does this compare to your reaction to movies adapted from books you have read?

3. Describe the front of the place where you live in only twenty words. Describe your bedroom in fifteen words. Describe yourself in ten without using any colors or numbers.

NAMES SHOULD BE A REFLECTION OF CHARACTER

It's no accident that the fur-loving, puppy-hating villainess of *101 Dalmatians* is named Cruella DeVil. You've not only got "cruel" in her first name but "devil" in the last. On the flip side, it's no coincidence that the object of affection for wacky inventor Caractacus Potts' (kinda sounds like "crackpot", doesn't it?) in *Chitty Chitty Bang Bang* is Truly Scrumptious, a woman as sweet as confectionery. In *National Treasure*, hero Benjamin Gates' middle name is Franklin. Coincidence? In *The African Queen*, Humphrey Bogart plays an unconventional rogue named Charlie Allnut; in *Toy Story*, Buzz Lightyear is an astronaut; Holly Golightly is the free-spirited heroine of *Breakfast at Tiffany's*; in *The Princess Diaries*, Clarisse is a name more befitting a regal queen than if she had shown up and introduced herself to granddaughter Mia as "Gert"; the reference to "Ethel Thayer" in *On Golden Pond* sets up the patriarch's line, "Thounds like I have a lithp."

In choosing first and last names for the characters in your script, it's important to select those that will subliminally convey strengths or weaknesses, stir curiosity, conjure favorable/negative associations, or elicit a chuckle. The latter is often used, for instance, when the moniker suggests the opposite of the persona who owns it, e.g., "Sunny" for a person who is always brooding or "Tiny" for a guy who is absolutely enormous.

If you're writing a period piece, it's also essential to have a familiarity with the names that were in vogue during that time. You wouldn't, for example, call a medieval knight "JJ" or attach a name like "Corky Sue" to a heroine in ancient Greece. Nor should you give characters names that are similar-sounding to one another (e.g., Felicia, Alicia, Lucretia) unless the intent of such similarity *is* to confuse your audience.

LOOK & LEARN

There are a number of library, bookstore and Internet resources available for screenwriters who want to ascribe clever and historically/ethnically/regionally plausible names to the characters who people their scripts. Check these out for ideas:

- *The Secret Universe of Names: The Dynamic Interplay of Names and Destiny* by Roy Feinson

- *American Given Names: Their Origin and History* by George Rippey Stewart

- *New Dictionary of American Family Names* by Elsdon C. Smith

- *www.lowchensaustralia.com/names/medievalnames.htm* (a great source for medieval, ancient, ethnic and mythological names)

- *www.ssa.gov/OACT/babynames/* (popular baby names — listed by state — between 1880 and 2004)

- *www.behindthename.com/top/* (the origin of some of the world's most popular first names)

- *http://surnames.behindthename.com/* (the origin of some of the world's most popular last names)

Additional lists can be found by doing a Google or Amazon.com search on "popular names," "surnames," "baby names," or "foreign names."

BRAINSTORMERS

1. Who are your three favorite movie villains? What do their names suggest to you about their personalities? If you wanted to turn each of these into good guys but could only change their first name *or* last name (not both!), what would you call them? (Example: Is Darth Vader as menacing if his first name is Elmo or Joey?)

2. You have decided to become a superhero. What (new) superhero name would you adopt and what would it tell the world about your particular powers?

3. What are the names of the characters in the film you want to write? How did you choose them and what do they say about their respective personalities?

A CHARACTER'S ACTIONS SAY MORE THAN HIS OR HER WORDS

If you caught your best friend in a lie and he or she promised you that it would never happen again, would you believe it? What if, only a week later, you witnessed this person doing the very same thing that you had been assured was past history? What value would all of those earnest and pleading pledges hold for you now?

The old expression that "actions speak louder than words" is just as true in stories that unfold on a movie screen. Film, after all, is a visual medium. We don't go to a show to watch the actors talk; we go to the show to watch them physically *do* something. This is important to remember as you start to develop your screenplay projects. Too often there is a tendency for writers to explain everything to the audience through dialogue that could be better conveyed through action, body language and nuance.

When Alfred Hitchcock made the observation that the measure of a good movie was one that could be watched with the sound off, he was referring to the principle of "Show, Don't Tell." Specifically, we should be able to follow the storyline and basic relationships without having them lengthily explained to us in voice overs or character conversations. While there may be a handful of details we miss during such "soundless" review, they're not the primary essence of the plot.

It's also crucial to keep in mind just how much information we communicate to one another through non-verbal behavior. Professional studies have shown, in fact, that only 7% of what we convey to someone is through the use of actual words; the rest is divided between tone of voice, gestures, posture/body language. (This advice applies to all those job interviews you're going to go on, too!)

LOOK & LEARN

There are some actors who can crack us up just by raising an eyebrow or issuing a smirk. Steve Martin is one of them. So is Robin Williams. To this list I'd also add one of my own favorites: the late Peter Sellers. In 1968, he appeared in *The Party* as a painfully shy but polite actor from India named Hrundi V. Bakshi. Bakshi is a walking disaster on the backlot of a movie where he's cast as an extra. He's so bad at everything (including blowing up the set) the director orders him fired. Instead, he receives an invitation to a glam Hollywood party where he sets off an accidental chain of events resulting in total chaos. What's fun and instructive about this film is how much Sellers conveys through physicality while at the same time arousing empathy from all of us who have ever felt like a social klutz.

BRAINSTORMERS

1. Have a friend, parent or teacher pick out a film you've never seen before. (Make sure they don't let you read the synopsis or anything about it first!) Watch the whole thing with the sound off, and then explain the story as you perceived it. How accurate were you in determining the plot and character relationships?

2. Go to a neighborhood café or coffee house. Situate yourself where you have a casual view of occupants across the room but can't hear their conversations. Without staring (or stalking!), jot down your observations regarding age, clothing, accessories and body language. Compose a short essay in which you give them names, explain their relationship and tell us what they were talking about.

3. Could the film you want to write be understood by an audience if they were watching it without any sound? Why or why not?

SOMETIMES THE AUDIENCE NEEDS TO KNOW MORE THAN THE CHARACTERS

A former boss of mine used to routinely sit in front of his television set during weekend football games and yell at his team whenever they fumbled the ball. "It's not as if they can actually *hear* you, dear," his wife would remark.

Moviegoers do pretty much the same thing — although probably on a quieter level — as they watch the characters up on the screen enter relationships and situations that are ultimately going to prove hazardous to their lives.

Don't they *know* this is the same woods where werewolves have been sighted?!

Don't they *know* there's a monster lurking down in the cellar?!

Don't they *know* the cute guy next door is actually a psychopath with an ax?!

Well, of *course* they don't know any of these things. It would make for a much shorter movie if they simply dialed "911" or moved to a safer neighborhood. What stretches out the story is that they are not only oblivious to the danger but that we, as the spectators, have absolutely no way to warn them about what's coming.

This "outside insider" knowledge, of course, is a useful screenwriting device for creating audience engagement in that it doesn't just get them speculating "what would I do if *I* were in that scene" but also allows them to experience two diametrically opposed feelings at the same time toward the fictional characters. The first, of course, is empathy — the ability to mentally relate to what someone else is going through. The second state is superiority — the smug recognition that if they had just listened to our advice, they wouldn't have gotten themselves into this particular mess to begin with.

Audiences like to feel smart. Let them. (Just don't make your players *too* stupid.)

LOOK & LEARN

In *Ghost*, the character of Sam Wheat is killed before he can expose a money laundering scheme involving one of his pals at the investment firm where they both work. It was this so-called friend, in fact, who arranged for Sam's murder. This film is a great example of the concept you just studied because its audience is clued in to the following information:

- Sam's spirit is trying to protect (and communicate with) Mollie.

- Oda Mae is really channeling Sam's voice.

- Mollie is in danger from the friend who had Sam killed.

- Neither Mollie nor Sam can move on until a final connection is made. For Mollie, it's knowing that Sam really loved her; for Sam, it's knowing that Mollie's life will finally be safe.

BRAINSTORMERS

1. Identify three films you've seen in which the audience was several steps ahead of the people in the plot. What methods did the screenwriter use to create this lack of awareness? (For example, were the characters in an isolated environment and, thus, didn't know that their houseguest was actually an escaped prisoner?

2. You've been sworn not tell a certain secret to your best friend. Your rationale, however, is that if he or she *guesses* it on their own, it's not exactly like breaking your word. Decide on what the secret is, then explain how you would go about dropping clues that could enable him/her to figure it out. (*Note*: This is a really fun classroom exercise in which everyone except the "friend" knows what you're cryptically trying to communicate.)

3. In the film you want to write, what secret(s) will your audience have that the characters themselves won't? Describe how you will keep this information from being discovered until it is (1) too late or (2) absolutely necessary.

SOMETIMES THE CHARACTERS NEED TO KNOW MORE THAN THE AUDIENCE

One of the cardinal rules of storytelling in any medium is that it's never fair to withhold information from an audience that might have allowed them to solve the mystery or conflict on their own. That's not to say, however, that a writer can't mirthfully lead them astray with red herrings, subplots or a "McGuffin." This latter word came into filmmaking vocabulary courtesy of its master, Alfred Hitchcock. In simple terms, a McGuffin is whatever *seems* to be important to the characters but is actually just a foil to distract an audience from the real plot. In *Psycho*, for instance, the $40,000 stolen by Marion Crane is simply a McGuffin to move her into the creepy world of Norman Bates. Once she steps into the shower, the embezzled funds are never mentioned again, quietly vaporizing the significance we as the audience initially attached to them.

There are also instances in which screenwriters have characters play their cards close to the chest and yet engage in decisions and actions that — by the story's end — are revealed to be consistent with everything else they have demonstrated from the outset. While we are momentarily surprised we weren't privy to their private thoughts, we are nonetheless satisfied that the writer hasn't pulled any punches.

This is poignantly demonstrated in *Robin & Marian* in which Sean Connery as the aged hero of Sherwood Forest discovers that his lady fair, played by Audrey Hepburn, has slipped a potion into both of their goblets that will render them lifeless. Wisely, she recognizes that neither she nor her beloved will ever know as glorious a day as those that have passed. She never clues *us* in on her end game but, at the end, we still accept it.

After all, who really knew him — and loved him — better than she did?

LOOK & LEARN

In *The Sting*, an elaborate charade is put into play which will not only divest the villain, Doyle Lonnegan, of a lot of money but also avenge the death of Hooker and Gondorff's fellow grifter, Luther. So successful is the ruse they enact that when an astonished audience sees Hooker and Gondorff mortally wounded on the floor of the casino, it's as willing as Lonnegan, Lt. Snyder and FBI Agent Polk to believe both men are "dead."

In *The Cherokee Kid*, the character of Isaiah (Sinbad) is bound and determined to avenge the death of his brother, Jedediah, in a showdown with The Undertaker (Gregory Hines). What's kept from us, however, is that The Undertaker *is* Jedediah.

And, of course, let's not forget the layers of secrecy inherent throughout the *Star Wars* saga. George Lucas knew the story's destination all along; he just played it coy in sharing glimpses of the map.

BRAINSTORMERS

1. Identify three films you've seen in which the characters knew more than they were revealing to the audience. What methods did the writer use to either shroud the truth or set up distractions to shift your focus? Do you feel the trickery was well done or clumsily contrived? Explain your answer.

2. Have you ever heard of Charlie Parkhurst? This real-life stagecoach driver in the Old West would make an intriguing and secretive character for a movie. Your assignment is to research who Charlie Parkhurst was and write a short, first-person essay about Charlie's first day on the job.

3. In the film you want to write, what is your plot's biggest surprise going to be?

MOTIVATION AND REDEMPTION

"But what's my motivation?!" many an actor laments when he or she can't understand why a particular action is taking place. Silly as that sounds, it all gets back to whether the writer has adequately justified a character's decisions and actions through *previous* decisions and actions. In film — as in real life — people never do things just for the heck of it. They do things because (1) it would never occur to them to do anything else and (2) they have a goal in mind that can only be achieved through one specific course of action. What this means is that motivation and redemption are joined at the hip insofar as whatever drives a character forward is contingent on the sole intent of reaching a finish line that will ultimately validate all of his or her hard work and beliefs.

Let's equate this for a moment to doing well on tests in school.

The "payoff" of higher grades is acceptance to a great college and, from there, acceptance into a well-paying job. In this scenario, redemption is synonymous with reward for all of the sacrifices (e.g., not partying with your friends past curfew) that allowed you to stay focused on your academic objectives. Without any motivation (e.g., "School? Who cares?"), there's neither a mechanism nor a measurement in place for a character to transcend fears and limitations.

In film, redemption often relates to some earlier failing on the part of the protagonist to prevent something bad from happening. Henceforth, his or her motivation is to either *prevent* the terrible whatever from ever occurring again or to *avenge* the original whatever. In achieving that goal, the character is not only forgiven for past failings but is allowed to move forward to a higher state of grace.

LOOK & LEARN

In *Life is Beautiful*, protagonist Guido Orefice's only weapons against his Nazi captors are his imagination and sense of humor. He uses both in a dangerous bid to protect his young son, Giosué, from the atrocities of the concentration camp to which they've been sent. By convincing Giosué that they are playing an elaborate game (with a full-size tank as the prize for the most "points" accrued), every scene supports Guido's single-minded motivation to do whatever it takes to keep his son from harm. By the final credits, Guido succeeds in accomplishing this goal even though it is at the cost of his own life. Guido's death is a product of violence but, at the same time, his soul is finally at peace — redeemed for all past transgressions — by delivering on the pledge he made to his heart. With the arrival of the Allies, Giosué is even the recipient of the coveted prize his father had promised him when their "game" began: a ride on a real tank.

BRAINSTORMERS

1. What is it that you believe in more strongly than anything else? How and when did this belief first come about? Who or what influences its continued existence in your life? Have you ever had this belief challenged by someone? What was the outcome? Provide your answers in a 500-word essay.

2. Complete this sentence: "I have never felt free to _____." Imagine that this is a character's declaration at the beginning of a movie. In a brief synopsis, tell us what will occur to release (and ultimately redeem) this person from his/her limits by the story's end.

3. In the film you want to write, identify the motivating forces that compel your protagonist to take risks in pursuit of a quest to change the status quo.

A SCRIPT IS NO PLACE FOR WORDS THAT JUST RAMBLE

In 1967, a musical called *You're a Good Man, Charlie Brown* (based on Charles Schulz's comic strip) debuted off-Broadway. Of particular note — and relevant to the subject of this chapter — is an ensemble number entitled "The Book Report" in which Lucy, Linus, Schroeder and Charlie Brown each have to write 100 words about the story of "Peter Rabbit." Lucy proceeds to use as much verbiage as possible ("They were very, very, very, very, very, very happy to be home") while Schroeder uses his essay as a forum to discuss a book he liked much better: "Robin Hood." What these two approaches serve to illustrate is the all too common habit of (1) using more words than are necessary or (2) wandering off on a path totally unrelated to the story at hand.

If you're going to write movies, this is a bad habit you can't afford to fall into. Why? Because each page of your script equals one minute of screen-time. Whether you're writing a fifteen-minute (fifteen-page) short or a two-hour (120 page) feature, every scene description needs to embrace brevity and every line of dialogue needs to accomplish a purpose. Unlike a book — which is meant to be *read* — a script is more like the blueprint of a house that has yet to be *built*. Unlike life — which unfolds slowly — a movie has only a short window of time to deliver its message. Thus, you can't waste space *or* time on anything that doesn't contribute to the film's theme and to the foundation, support and resolution of the conflict.

The economical word-play of screenwriting in order to maximize the value of every line and scene will be hard at first. Mastering this technique, however, will carry over into other aspects of your writing such as college entrance exams, freelance articles for magazines and newspapers, and essays or contests that have word-count limits.

LOOK & LEARN

In order to *write* movies, you need to *watch* movies. This same rule not only holds true for books and plays but for any craft or sport in which you'd like to excel. In the course of developing your own unique voice and style, you need to be familiar with what your predecessors (and competitors!) have already contributed. In this chapter's discussion about using as few words as possible to convey your vision to an audience, it's important that you study a variety of films and compare what they initially looked like on paper before the cameras ever got rolling. The following websites allow you to download scripts of your favorite movies and appreciate this minimalist form of writing:

- Script Crawler: *www.scriptcrawler.com*
- Drew's Script-O-Rama: *www.script-o-rama.com*
- Script Pimp: *www.scriptpimp.com*

Additional scripts can be found by typing "Free Screenplays" in your search engine.

BRAINSTORMERS

1. Lincoln's "Gettysburg Address" is 278 words. The fictitious director of an equally fictitious 1860s film company has told you this particular monologue is too long and needs to be cut down to 150. Your assignment (as a Civil War screenwriter) is to trim the speech without compromising the essence of its message.

2. What's the most recent movie you've seen? Describe the entire thing from start to finish… in only 100 words.

3. Pick any essay or short story you have written in the last three months. Count how many words it contains. Rewrite the same story but use half the number of words as the original text. Discuss what this exercise revealed to you about your writing style.

DINING AT THE SPEED OF LIGHT

What is wrong with the following scene?

> MEGAN and DANIEL are shown to their table by a WAITER.
>
> WAITER
> What would you like for dinner?
>
> MEGAN
> I'll have the salmon filet with wild rice
> and the carrot medley.
>
> DANIEL
> Make mine a steak — well done — with a
> baked potato and some spinach.
>
> The waiter exits.
>
> DANIEL
> So how was your day? Is your boss still a jerk?
>
> MEGAN
> Absolutely! It's practically his middle name.
>
> The waiter returns with their orders.
>
> WAITER
> Enjoy your entrees.

Did you figure it out? If one page of a script equals one minute of screen time, this has to be one of the *fastest* restaurants in town: in the space of only two lines, the order has been placed, cooked and brought to the table! Interestingly, this is one of the two most common mistakes new screenwriters make in food scenes. (The other one is indicating every time a character picks up a fork, sips a drink, chews and/or swallows.)

To resolve this, you can use intercuts with other scenes (the meal will have "progressed" with each return to the table), start the scene with the meal already half-consumed/ nearly over, or employ a dissolve (e.g., melting candles) to show that time has passed. As for excessive stage direction, I've yet to meet an actor who didn't know how to wield utensils and attack a free meal! Simply indicate: They eat their food.

LOOK & LEARN

An excellent restaurant scene for study can be found in *Moonstruck*, a romantic comedy that can be downloaded for free from *www.scriptcrawler.com*. In the first-act scene at the Grand Ticino Italian restaurant, pay particular attention to the dynamics of Loretta and her reluctant beau, Johnny, university professor Perry and his young date, and Bobo and his fellow waiters. Another scene worth a look can be found later in the story when Rose Castorini, Loretta's mother, encounters the same professor at the same restaurant. The interactions and timing here are beautiful and crafted in such a way that none of the service feels rushed or artificial. After reading the scenes, rent the film to see how they were conveyed in "real" time.

BRAINSTORMERS

1. In *Tortilla Soup*, Hector Elizondo plays a retired Mexican-American chef with three grown daughters. Much of the action revolves around the dinner table. Using this film as a model, write a two-page dinner table scene involving the members of your own family and what they talk about while they're eating.

2. *Home for the Holidays* is a comedy in which everything that could possibly go wrong at Thanksgiving dinner turns out to do exactly that. What's the worst holiday dinner you've ever had? In a 100-word essay, describe how you would incorporate this into a short film.

3. Your character is planning to break up with his date at a fancy restaurant. Should this conversation occur (1) right after they order; (2) halfway through the meal; or (3) during dessert? If you only had two pages for the entire dining scene, how would you write it? What will be the scene immediately following this one?

FANCY FOOTWORK AND FISTICUFFS

Sooner or later your hero and villain will square off and utter those immortal words, "This town/galaxy/boardroom ain't big enough for the two of us."

What happens then?

If you're new to writing fight scenes for a screenplay, one of two things is likely to occur:

1. You'll describe every single step, feint, punch, bob, weave, and even include the trajectory of splashed blood and the precise number of teeth that get knocked out.

2. You'll type: "They fight for about twenty minutes or so."

The problem with the first scenario is that copious detail not only eats up a lot of space on the page but suggests to a prospective director that you don't think he/she knows how to choreograph an intense scene that involves a lot of physicality. The more that you try to "direct on paper" and dictate every move, the longer it takes to read the script. This, in turn, can slow the momentum of the plot.

The second approach ignores the fact that one page = one minute and secretly pads extra length in the final product. It's also the equivalent of writing obscure instruction such as, "The actors ad lib for awhile." At a minimum we need to be able to visualize whether the opponents are evenly matched, what their respective advantages are, and whether any props are being employed. Simply saying "they fight" doesn't show us *how*.

Always remember that a good fight scene is minimalist in its written description, relating only those elements that are pertinent to the outcome or to subsequent scenes.

LOOK & LEARN

The description of fight scenes varies from one genre to the next. The writing is influenced as well by whether the film was written for a specific star with specific physical skills (e.g., the comedic styling of martial arts expert Jackie Chan). The following films are good examples for study and can be downloaded from websites such as 499 Movie Scripts (*http://67.118.51.201//bol/MovDsply.cfm*), Awesome Films (*www.awesomefilmcom*), Script Crawler (*www.scriptcrawler.com*), and Daily Script (*www.dailyscript.com/scripts*).

- *Crouching Tiger, Hidden Dragon*
- *Die Hard*
- *Rocky*
- *The Princess Bride*
- *Gladiator*
- *Rush Hour*
- *Pirates of the Caribbean*
- *The Avengers*
- *The Matrix*
- *12 Monkeys*

BRAINSTORMERS

1. What's the best movie fight scene you've ever seen? What made it compelling, frightening, or funny? Download the script and study how the scene was written.

2. Write a two-page comedic fight scene between Spiderman and Superman. Halfway through this fight, a third superhero intervenes. Who is it and how does this impact the outcome?

3. It's snack-time at the daycare center and a roomful of four-year-olds are getting restless. Uh-oh. Someone forgot to buy cookies and juice drinks. In a two-page scene, show us how the pint-sized protesters get ugly.

FOR "REEL" TALK TO SOUND "REAL", YOU NEED VOCAL VARIETY

Do you have younger brothers and sisters? Do you have grandparents? Do you have friends at school who learned to speak English as a second language? Do either or both of your parents work in a specialized field with its own unique lingo?

I'm going to make a guess that no two individuals in this small sampling talk exactly the same way. Am I right? Education, ethnicity, gender, experience and regional slang and dialects all influence how words are going to come out of our mouths. The same is true of the fictional characters that you put in your screenplay.

Oddly enough, however, a newbie writer often gives all of his or her players exactly the *same* voice; specifically, the voice of the author. If you were to cover up the names of the characters, for example, it might be hard to distinguish the speakers from one another. They also attempt to either mimic real-life conversation — complete with all of the "um's, ah's, duh's, hmm's" — or compose "Queen's English" dialogue that would be better suited to the pages of a book (e.g., "Would you be ever so kind, Joe, as to please pass the butter to your sister, Margaret, when you have a moment?").

Although writing is a solitary craft, there's a big difference between reading your script silently to yourself and assigning friends to read all of the roles out loud. What the latter will enable you to do is to "hear" whether the lines sound natural and are consistent with the personality, education, upbringing, etc. that you have ascribed to each character.

As you continue to download and read screenplays of existing films, you'll see how what has been set down in print translates to dialogue that flows naturally, economically and sounds "real" to the ear.

LOOK & LEARN

In the 2001 film *I Am Sam*, Sean Penn turns in a compelling perform-ance as a mentally retarded man who fathers a little girl and, as a sin-gle parent, attempts to raise her while working a minimum-wage job at Starbucks. By the time little Lucy is seven, her IQ has already sur-passed his. This concerns the child welfare authorities who think that Lucy would be better off in foster care than with the dad who loves her more than anything.

   This is a great film for studying dialogue. Pay attention to the respective vocabulary, syntax and analytical abilities inherent in the characters of Sam, Rita, Lucy and Annie. What has the screenwriter done to make each of their voices unique?

BRAINSTORMERS

1. *Galaxy Quest* is about a group of actors in a sci-fi TV series who are mistaken by aliens as the real thing. Based on how they each speak, identify which character is (1) the best educated; (2) the least educated; (3) the most sincere; (4) the most clueless; (5) the least egocentric; (6) the most resilient. Explain your answers.

2. How characters talk is often influenced by who they are talking *to*. In this exercise, you have just broken a valuable lamp. Demonstrate how you would explain this accident to: (1) your mother; (2) your best friend; (3) a three-year-old; (4) a neighbor whose knowledge of English is limited; (5) a minister.

3. Tape record a conversation between two friends. Transcribe this tape word-for- word. Explain why or why not this verbatim tran-scription would work in a screenplay. Choose two other friends to read this conversation out loud exactly as written and time it. How much information does it convey within this timeframe?

CHARACTERS SHOULDN'T USE DIALOGUE TO EXPLAIN THINGS TO EACH OTHER THAT THEY ALREADY KNOW

When you're a young and inquisitive wizard like Harry Potter, a cloak of invisibility can be a pretty nifty accessory for finding out information that others are determined to keep under wraps. Sometimes, however, you learn more than you wanted to know. In *Harry Potter and the Prisoner of Azkaban*, Harry overhears Professor McGonagall explaining to her tavern companions that the escaped wizard Sirius Black was not only the Potters' trusted friend but was Harry's godfather as well.

From our knowledge of the first film in which McGonagall and Dumbledore dropped Baby Harry off on his relatives' doorstep, we have to assume she's been keeping this tidbit under her pointed hat for at least the past thirteen years. Why, then, does she choose this moment to freely chat about it outside of Hogwarts? Because her target listener isn't Harry: it's the audience.

This example of poor exposition is provided to show that newbie screenwriters aren't the only ones who resort to the contrivance of divulging clues, strategies and relationships through conversations that would either already have transpired long before we got there or else exist as unspoken understandings between the players involved. Other samples of this flimsy explanatory device exist in scenes where:

- Criminals review their secret plans in copious detail so we can all follow along.

- Guests at a party are introduced to everyone else by their entire life story.

- Historical events are put in context for the audience by improbable chit-chat such as, "Napoleon, as you've probably heard, was exiled to Saint Helena last year after his second abdication and surrender to British warships…"

Bottom line: If it won't pass for plausible chatter, find a different way to reveal it to your viewers.

LOOK & LEARN

> ILSA
> I wasn't sure you were the same. Let's see,
> the last time we met…
>
> RICK
> Was La Belle Aurore.
>
> ILSA
> How nice you remembered. But, of course,
> that was the day the Germans marched into Paris.
>
> RICK
> Not an easy day to forget.
>
> ILSA
> No.
>
> RICK
> I remember every detail. The Germans wore gray,
> you wore blue.

Are Rick and Ilsa talking to each other or simply filling the rest of us in on the details of their last encounter? In *Casablanca*, the answer doesn't really matter because it fits the plausibility test; specifically, two star-crossed lovers reflecting on the defining moment that changed their lives forever. That it's also romantic goes without saying….

BRAINSTORMERS

1. If you were rewriting *Casablanca*, describe how you would reveal the same background information above to an audience differently than it was written.

2. Identify six different ways to reveal a character's name and occupation to the audience without another character having to make a formal introduction to a third party. Two examples to get you started: (1) A nameplate and title on the door of a character's office; (2) A radio DJ signing on or off the air.

3. In the film you want to write, how will you establish for the audience your main character's relationships to others in the story? How much "history" does he or she have with each of them? Is the past relevant to the plot? Why or why not?

DON'T USE A VOICE OVER IF A VISUAL WOULD SAY MUCH MORE

One of the mainstays of educational films for school and documentaries for public television is the voice of an off-screen narrator who neatly puts everything into its proper historical, sociological or scientific context for us (e.g., "Here we see the female *Libellula depressa* doing a dance to attract a mate"). We accept such periodic intrusions because (1) we're watching this material in order to enhance our knowledge of the subject matter; and/or (2) we might otherwise have no clue what it is we're looking at.

Voice overs also find their way into feature films and shorts. Although they generally appear as a vocal prologue at the beginning of the story or at the very end as an epilogue, a film might utilize a narrator throughout if, for instance, it's a diary-style or retrospective story in which the feelings of the lead character (or sidelines observer) aren't easily expressed through physical action or dialogue with other players. Before you start using this technique, however, you need to ask yourself whether it's because:

1. You need to supply some brief background so that you can cut to the chase of the central conflict and have it quickly understood.

2. Certain scenes would be cost-prohibitive to fully enact.

3. A voice over is an omniscient way to explain existing relationships.

4. You're feeling lazy and would rather just tell the audience what's going on than write a scene that would actually show them.

Reasons 1 through 3 are acceptable uses of a voice over. Reason 4 is not. Film is a visual medium. Accordingly, you should never use a voice over to feed an audience information that could be better expressed — and remembered — through vivid imagery.

LOOK & LEARN

In *While You Were Sleeping*, the voice over of Lucy introduces herself as a starry-eyed romantic who longs to see the world but has somehow never managed to get much farther than working in a Chicago transit toll booth. We also learn she is secretly in love with a handsome man who catches the same train everyday but, thus far, has never even noticed her. With this background quickly out of the way, we can move to the heart of the story: A case of mistaken identity that finds Lucy engaged to the (comatose) man of her dreams but romantically attracted to his brother.

In Neil Simon's *Lost in Yonkers* (adapted from his Broadway play of the same name), the voice over serves to introduce us to the hardships of the 1940s and the lifestyle adjustments that young Jay and Artie need to make when sent to live with their grumpy Grandma Kurnitz and ditzy Aunt Bella.

BRAINSTORMERS

1. Identify three movies in which voice overs were used. Using the criteria on the previous page, explain why this technique was effective in advancing each plot.

2. In *National Treasure*, young Ben's grandfather relates the legend of the Knights Templar and their connection to the Gates family. Would this background have been effective if related to us without the accompanying, historic visuals (in other words, simply told to Ben in the attic as a story)? Why or why not?

3. Do you plan to use any voice overs in the film you want to write? If yes, explain what this technique will accomplish in terms of set-up, budget and emotional perspective. If no, explain why a voice over wouldn't work for your storyline.

DREAMS AND·FLASHBACKS

Scenario 1: Your female lead is sitting in study hall when the new foreign exchange student, José, walks in. Although their eyes meet for only a second, she's instantly besotted. The classroom is suddenly transformed into a wedding chapel. She's wearing a bridal gown and carrying a bouquet as the angelic strains of a chorus fill the air. Just as he holds out his hand to her, the strident sound of a school bell snaps her back to reality.

Scenario 2: Your protagonist is in a foreign city, riding the local train. An older lady boards and he can't help but do a double-take as soon as he sees her. *I know that woman! But from <u>where</u>?* Since he's never been in this city before, he realizes it has to be from sometime and somewhere in the past. And then he remembers. We as an audience know that he's remembering because we're suddenly seeing a younger version of himself *and* a younger version of the mystery lady who turns out to have been his babysitter.

In both set-ups, the plot takes a temporary time-out to invite an audience into a character's fantasy world or provide "history" that an author feels is necessary to better understand the current conflict. These segues are shown through transitions such as DISSOLVE, FADE, WIPE — camera cues that substitute one image with another and are placed at the far right margin in the script like this:

DISSOLVE TO:

Flashbacks are also conveyed via title cards on screen; e.g., "10 Years Ago." Morphs and match cuts are popular, too. In these effects, the present-day image (1) "melts" into a younger/older one or (2) an object such as a modern snapshot held by a character is lowered to reveal a "vintage" shot of the same subject and from the same angle. *Warning*: Use such effects sparingly or they will slog the pacing of your story.

LOOK & LEARN

In the 1962 version of *The Manchurian Candidate*, director John Frankenheimer uses an interesting flashback technique to demonstrate the Communist brainwashing tactics used on Raymond Shaw and the members of his platoon. Specifically, the flashback appears *simultaneously* with the conversation between Laurence Harvey and Frank Sinatra. Take note as well of the opening dream sequence that sets the plot in motion as well as the flashback dinner scene with Josie and her father, Senator Jordan.

Another film worth studying for its seamless incorporation of flashbacks is *Citizen Kane* in which associates of the enigmatic deceased tycoon are asked to reflect on what kind of person he was and why his dying word was "Rosebud."

BRAINSTORMERS

1. You are making a film about the life of the late Rosa Parks, an icon of the American civil rights movement. Assuming that she is relating the story in her senior years, explain what techniques you would use to introduce the flashback scene of her refusing to give up her seat on the bus.

2. What is the latest dream you've had? Was it funny? Frightening? Profound? In a 100-word essay, explain how you would incorporate this dream into a short film as a way to yield insight into the personality and/or fears of the main character.

3. In *Sidekicks*, an asthmatic youth named Barry spends a lot of time imagining that he is sharing adventures with his favorite action hero (Chuck Norris). In your own daydreams, who do you see yourself spending time with, what are the two of you doing, and how could you successfully incorporate this fantasizing into a short film plot?

MOOD-SETTING MONTAGES

In the previous chapter you learned how dreams and flashbacks respectively provide us with insights on where the characters would like to be and where they've already been. Both devices help us to understand what makes them tick and, accordingly, what governs their decision making insofar as resolving the central conflict. These scenes are usually comprised of character interactions through dialogue and a series of shots related to a specific time period in either the future or the past.

Contrast this to a series of present-moment shots *without* dialogue which is called a "montage." Usually underscored with music or solo narration, the purpose of a montage is to evoke a particular theme or emotion for the audience. The opening shots of a film, for instance, are often used as a virtual postcard to prep us for the type of story that is going to unfold. Montages are set up at the left slug line just like intercut scenes:

BEGIN MANHATTAN MONTAGE
    1) FIFTH AVENUE — Bustling SHOPPERS with Gucci, Prada, Saks bags
    2) RADIO CITY MUSIC HALL — a crowd of shutterbug TOURISTS
    3) CENTRAL PARK — Romantic COUPLES and boisterous FAMILIES
    4) TIMES SQUARE — Taxicab gridlock at rush hour
END MANHATTAN MONTAGE

Montages are also used during a story as a series of quick cuts to show characters preparing for a date, experiencing the loneliness of a bad break-up, or — in a humorous vein — reinventing themselves via different hairstyles and wardrobes. For historical works and documentaries, montages often integrate live action with photos and stand-alone props.

LOOK & LEARN

The opening scenes of *Casablanca* are an excellent example of a montage that is supplemented by a newscast-style voice over. This not only sets up the exotic North African backdrop (a locale which, mind you, was very exciting to movie-going audiences in the pre-Internet era) but establishes from the outset the desperation of European refugees hoping to secure the necessary exit visas to leave the country.

Another example to look at is the midway makeover of Loretta (Cher) in *Moonstruck*. Her transformation from dowdy to dazzling is orchestrated in only a few short sentences and illustrates how "less is more" in communicating through a simple montage what would otherwise take multiple pages to describe in master scenes and dialogue.

BRAINSTORMERS

1. Do you live in a big city? A small town? A rural community? If your current address were the establishing shot of a feature film, identify six to ten scenes for a montage that would evoke its true sense of character for an audience. What type of music would you use underneath? Why (or why not) would you add narration?

2. What is your favorite music video? Turn the sound off as you watch it. What emotions do the visuals of this video convey to you? Are these emotions consistent with the message of the lyrics themselves?

3. A TV network is launching a nature program and has hired you to develop a sixty-second promo for them. Using what you have just learned about montage, describe what visuals, music and voice-over narration you would use to get audiences excited about tuning into this new and exciting series.

SAVE THE BIG SPEECHES FOR WHEN THEY'LL REALLY COUNT

Do you have friends or relatives who tend to talk more than anyone else? When they start a story, do you think to yourself, "Argh! I won't be able to escape from this for the next hour and a half"? Do you dread starting a conversation with someone because you know that getting a word in edgewise will be like trying to thread a sewing machine while it's running? Even the most interesting people we know can become tiresome if all they do is talk, talk, talk and never allow for input from those who are with them.

The same applies to the characters in your script. While actors certainly love roles that allow them a meaty, Oscar-worthy monologue to sink their teeth into, the impact of such a speech will be hugely diluted if it turns out to be one of seventeen spoken by the same character. Do you really want your audience to sink into their seats with a groan and murmur, "Oh no, here's comes the yakker again"? Of course not!

Nor do you want characters to talk to each other in chunky, half-page paragraphs instead of crisp one-liners. Rarely in real-life conversations do paragraph dialogs occur. Even if one person is holding court and telling a long-winded story, his or her speech is frequently interrupted and interspersed with remarks from the other parties present. It may only be something brief such as "Really?", "How come?", "No way!", or "Go on", but it all serves to break up long stretches of yakkiness on the part of a solo speaker.

It's also important to note that a character's Big Speech generally falls somewhere past the halfway mark of the script and is a culmination (and pay off) for the audience who has been watching this person's emotions and stakes gradually build. If you place the Big Speech too early in the story, it's tough for the character to ever top it later on.

LOOK & LEARN

Have you ever been the captain of a sports team that was squaring off with a nemesis that was bigger, stronger and liked to cheat? Your teammates probably looked to you to say something inspirational to fuel their desire to get out there and win. In such moments, you could appreciate Captain Jack Aubrey in *Master and Commander* whose stirring speech — precipitating his crew's encounter with the French ship they had been chasing across two oceans — sums up with the following words:

> *Even crippled, she will still be dangerous … like a wounded beast. Captain Howard and the marines will sweep their weather deck with swivel gun and musket fire from the tops … and try and even the odds for us before we board. They mean to take us as a prize … and we are worth more to them undamaged. Their greed … will be their downfall. England is under threat of invasion … and though we be on the far side of the world, this ship is our home. This ship … is England. So it's every hand to his rope or gun! Quick's the word and sharp's the action! After all … surprise is on our side.*

After a kicker of a pep-talk like that, you can bet that the French were toast.

BRAINSTORMERS

1. Identify three films in which one of the characters had a Big Speech. What was the plot circumstance and physical placement of that speech in the story and why was it effective or ineffective?

2. How well do you know your Oscars? Go to the official Academy Awards database at *www.oscars.org/awardsdatabase*. Click on SEARCH in the left-hand toolbar which takes you to a screen where you can find out who won what in any given year. In a random sample of three Best Actors and three Best Actresses, identify which ones had roles containing a Big Speech.

3. Will any of the characters in your film have a Big Speech? Why or why not?

ACTORS SHOULD NEVER BE LEFT TO AD-LIB

What's wrong with this scene description:

The doctors discuss the pros and cons of proceeding with the surgery and then head downstairs to have lunch where most of them order sandwiches and soup.

How about this one?

The peasants chatter amongst themselves about whether it's better to storm the Count's castle door with a big log or light torches and set fire to the entire building. They take a vote, decide the log is a good idea and someone volunteers to go cut down a tree.

The answer is the same in both examples; the writers have left the actors to come up with their own lines of dialogue. Big mistake. In the first place, while many actors are gifted at improvisation and use it in live performances to cover up mistakes and missed cues, their expectation in a film is that the script in their hands won't call for them to do anything except emote. In the second place, an actor who *can* be brilliant off-the-cuff may be a little too inventive and introduce material that doesn't fit the plot.

Even if you're feeling lazy or aren't well versed on the specialized lingo of your fictional hero's career, you should never resort to shortcuts that require someone else to plug up the gaps. Just because someone is *playing* a doctor, for instance, doesn't mean he or she can casually rabbit on about subdural hematomas and myocardial infarctions as "filler" until the next scene. If a conversation is important enough to be in the story, it's the writer's job to provide the lines that need to be spoken.

Likewise, you should never insert directorial comments such as "This might be a good place to maybe blow up something in the background like you did in such-and-such." Directors — just like actors — really don't like to do other people's homework for them.

LOOK & LEARN

Crowd scenes present an interesting challenge to screenwriters in that it would be impossible to assign specific lines of dialogue to everyone present. Where the scene takes place at a sports event or in a city where multitudes are fleeing an approaching comet, the direction is usually minimal; i.e., the crowd screams. Where snippets of words are required, however, writers comply by penning six to eight lines in one block such as:

> ANGRY MOB
> Kill the monster!
> We want his blood!
> Kill him now!

During filming, extras alternate in shouting these lines out. And speaking of extras, fewer of them are being used these days in crowd scenes. Not only are they supplanted by cut-outs and mannequins but by three-dimensional graphics as well.

BRAINSTORMERS

1. It's lunch hour in the cafeteria and the cooks have run out of tacos. Your classmates are in an uproar. Write a block of eight "angry mob" lines you think they would shout in protest. Get a big group together, give them instructions on alternating, and listen to how it sounds.

2. Using the same crowd, tell each of them to say the phrase "rubba-ka-bubble" over and over but not in unison with each other. This trick has been used in theater and film for years to mimic the din of a crowd without saying anything intelligible.

3. Watch any movie that has a scene with people talking at a party. How many individual lines can you pick out? Download a copy of the script and see how the writer actually described it.

WHAT WE SEE ISN'T ALWAYS WHAT WE GET

How we talk to parents and teachers is different from how we talk to our friends, our siblings, or total strangers. This is because of (1) the comfort level we feel in expressing our real feelings to them and (2) the appropriateness of the moment and environment. A remark made "in context" ascribes meaning within the parameters of a specific situation. When something is taken "out of context," the inference is made that the listener is applying the same meaning unilaterally. For example, you tell the geeky son of your dad's boss that you're happy he came to the party. Why? Because — in context — your dad and his boss are standing right there and you're just being polite. The son, however, reads more into this and — out of context — starts telling everyone you're a couple. Yikes!

While "context" deals with what seems to be going on at a surface level, "subtext" is everything that exists beneath. In an earlier chapter, you learned that a theme is the glue that holds your story together. Subtext is an element of that glue because it not only reiterates the core message of the film throughout but hints at the underlying (and sometimes contrary) meanings behind a character's actions and words.

Subtext is also conveyed through the use of visual symbolism. Interestingly, Mother Nature figures prominently in these scenarios as a creative way to mirror the combustibility, futility or frailty of human relationships. Whether it's through repeated intercuts showing an approaching hurricane, a parched landscape that can't sustain life, a river spilling over its banks or the violent eruption of a volcano, the selection and placement of these illustrative markers correspond to the unleashing of emotions, oftentimes at the expense of everything else in the vicinity.

LOOK & LEARN

Do you think that child stars and prodigies have a harder or easier life than kids their own age? This question is explored in *Searching for Bobby Fischer*, a film in which a young boy's sudden affinity for chess — and tutelage under two radically different masters — begs the question of whether we can control the gifts of talent bestowed upon us or whether those gifts will ultimately exert control over all that we do.

Inspired by the real-life journey of world chess champion Bobby Fischer, this script delivers subtext not only through the playing of the game itself but in a pivotal exchange between Max and the street-smart Vinnie. In your own words, apply the significance of this scene to your personal life and your dreams for the future.

BRAINSTORMERS

1. Describe an event in which something you said or did in the context of a particular moment was misconstrued by someone else. What were the consequences? How did you clear up the misunderstanding?

2. Identify three movies in which the background weather or environmental conditions served as subtext to character interactions. (*Note*: Films in which natural disasters *are* the central conflict don't count!)

3. Directors often use their films as a platform to advance personal philosophies and politics through the subtext of dialogue and symbolism. Who is your favorite director? Is there a pattern to his or her themes (e.g., Oliver Stone and conspiracy theories)? What do you feel is this person trying to communicate in a non-fiction fashion through the use of fictional characters and conflicts?

STEREOTYPES AND CHARACTER REVERSALS

When I was a geeky freshman, my parents sent me to modeling classes to learn poise. These were taught by a humorless woman who looked like Wallis Warfield Simpson, exhibited a fondness for pillbox hats and had a poodle named Bruce. At semester's end, one of my classmates wanted to have a tea at her parents' house. My mother forbade me to go, citing that protocol would have demanded me to reciprocate. In the vernacular of Long Island, my classmate was NOCD ("not our crowd, dear") and would have had my mother fretting about the possibilities of stolen silver. Yes, you guessed it: my classmate was of a different culture, a scenario which caused my mother to parrot the same ugly biases that had been felt by *her* parents. Interestingly, screenwriters exhibit a similar mindset when it comes to the prejudicial depiction of dumb blonds, miserly Scots, sleazy lawyers, Italian mobsters, etc.

While political correctness has done much to combat the perpetuation of global "isms" (racism, sexism, etc.), too often authors resort to typecasting as a lazy way to fill up space. In doing so, however, they inject predictability into these characters' actions (e.g., the blond will always do something stupid) and, thus, dilute a story's element of surprise. Arghghghgh! Development people groan whenever they encounter hackneyed stereotypes. In order to make them say "Wow!' instead, you need to employ the art of *reversals*, imbuing "types" with traits contrary to our expectations, e.g., a brainy blond, a sensitive biker who does needlepoint, an old lady who knows jujitsu, a redneck who plays classical music, a librarian who's a part-time bounty hunter. In short, don't bore us with characters whom generations of prejudice have lumped into false preconceptions.

LOOK & LEARN

The Color Purple, adapted from a novel by Alice Walker, is a powerful film that speaks volumes regarding the fragility — and indestructibility — of the human spirit. Through the eyes and poignant words of its central character, Celie, we see the cruelties wrought by racism and sexism against the unforgiving backdrop of the rural South in the early part of the twentieth century. Contrast this meek young woman's submissiveness to the more driven persona of Sofia (portrayed by Oprah Winfrey), a woman determined to live by her own rules. Pay close attention as well to the turning points which ultimately redefine the stereotypical roles and attitudes of Celie, Shug Avery and "Mister."

BRAINSTORMERS

1. Which do you feel perpetuate stereotypes more: sitcoms or TV dramas? Provide three examples from each to support your answer.

2. In 2005, Northeastern State University in Tahlequah, Oklahoma crowned Muriel Saunders their homecoming queen. And the point of this is what? Saunders was seventy-one years old and a forty-year cancer survivor. If this story were a film, what would it say to audiences about the vitality, popularity and gumption of senior citizens in a youth-oriented society? In a 100-word essay, explain why you believe Muriel beat out her younger competitors for the crown.

3. The following occupations are often portrayed in film and TV as stereotypes: hairdressers, truck drivers, bartenders, Hollywood agents, fast food clerks, school principals, fashion models, bank security guards. Pick one of them and create a reversal we wouldn't expect (e.g., a parking attendant who sings opera).

CONTEXT + SUBTEXT = DELIVERY

When you start to write character dialogue, you'll want to write it in such a way that whoever picks up the script will understand how you meant for the lines (and accompanying body language) to be delivered. What you *don't* want to do, however, is clutter up the page with so much direction (*angrily, sadly, sarcastically, happily*) that you end up (1) wasting space that could be better spent developing plot and characters or (2) insulting actors who will resent that you don't think they can figure out every nuance on their own, much less the film's underlying themes and subliminal messaging.

If you saw the line, "How did you get in here?" but there were no accompanying details about the scene or circumstances in which it appears — nor any underscored words for emphasis — you'd have no way of knowing the writer's intention or character's mindset. Should it be delivered in a hostile fashion? A nervous squeak? A seductive tease? Incredulous amazement? Unabashed delight? Is the party to whom this line is being delivered an intruder, an axe murderer, a spouse, a puppy, a best friend?

The context of a scene provides us with a framework relative to the emotions, dialogue and action contained within it. If the subtext is consistent with the context, there's little need to explain *how* a line should be delivered; we already know the characters' objectives and how their verbiage reflects those goals. If, however, the words themselves fit the circumstance but the speaker's motive is contrary, a few clues are permissible. For example, how often have you been told to apologize to a sibling? "I'm sorry" may be the words that come out but the inclusion of (*snidely*) or the glimpse of crossed fingers leaves no mistake of the actual feeling going on behind them.

LOOK & LEARN

In both the 1971 *Willy Wonka & the Chocolate Factory* and its 2005 remake, *Charlie & the Chocolate Factory*, the storyline unfolds in a fantasy environment that truly fits the definition of "eye candy." Within this colorfully extravagant and deliciously mouthwatering childhood dream, however, lurks a darker message that some could say borders on a pretty icky nightmare. How was the filmmakers' subtext and author Roald Dahl's original vision of the reclusive candy maker communicated visually and through seemingly unsophisticated dialogue?

BRAINSTORMERS

1. For each of the following lines, come up with three different contexts in which it could be used.

   - I don't have the money.
   - This is bad.
   - We have to do something.
   - It can't be true.
   - That train has left the station.
   - What can I do for you?
   - I don't want this.
   - Is this what I think it is?
   - Do you mind?
   - Can I trust you?

2. Would the delivery of each line be self-explanatory or would it require underscored words or parenthetical clues to hint at the subtext? Explain how you would make the meaning clear in each scene you have come up with.

3. What do *Willy Wonka/Charlie & the Chocolate Factory*, *Peter Pan*, *Pinocchio*, *The Polar Express*, and *The Wizard of Oz* have in common in terms of their respective subtext? Identify specific scenes in each film to support your answer. Why is fantasy an effective vehicle for delivering these subliminal themes?

ALWAYS KEEP THE "ACCENT" ON READABILITY

Let's pretend for a moment you're an actor who has been called to an audition. Rather than memorizing a monologue beforehand or being provided a preview copy of the script, you and your fellow actors will engage in a "cold" reading of the material. This means you only have one chance to deliver the words accurately and with the appropriate level of emotion. You open the script to a page designated by the casting director and here is your first speech, that of an opera singer named Rita Cavallini.

> "I am qvite sure dis is de las' time dat ve spik togedder — de las' time dat I look upon your face. An' so I vant to tell you jus' a lee-tle somet'in' — an' den — vell, mebbe I say good-bye. You are ver' kin' to t'ink of me so much, aftair all de trouble I 'ave bring. An' I t'ank you — I shall alvays be oblige'. But, dear, you ken forget me now. Eez all right. Your vork eez done."
>
> (From *Romance* – 1913 stage play subsequently adapted to a 1920 silent film and a 1930 film starring Greta Garbo.)

As helpful as the author is trying to be in spelling out all of Rita's lines phonetically, the result is the opposite. Not only is the delivery slowed down and stumbled through in the course of sounding out individual words but the meaning behind them is lost as well.

This is important to keep in mind if you want to incorporate regional dialects or foreign characters in your script. Each time you inject something that can't be read easily, it slogs the pace of the material and taxes the patience of the reader. Since whoever is cast in an accented role will already know how to do dialects or will be coached by a pro, you're better off simply saying "with Italian accent" and write the lines — with an occasional sprinkle of idioms or transposed words — in regular English.

LOOK & LEARN

Ang Lee's *Crouching Tiger, Hidden Dragon* is a spectacular martial arts film that seamlessly blends romance, mysticism, athleticism, ancient culture and themes of avenging family honor. So how exactly was the dialogue written if the entire thing takes place in a foreign land? You can see for yourself at *www.script-o-rama.com* by clicking on "Film Scripts" and scrolling down until you find the title in the left-hand column. Contrast this to films such as *Rush Hour* and *Rush Hour 2* which intercut the street-smart African American lingo of Chris Tucker (Carter) with the measured politeness of Hong Kong visitor Jackie Chan (Lee).

> *James Carter*: Couldn't help noticin' how she was staring at a brother.
> *Lee*: She never even looked at you.
> *James Carter*: You just jealous, Lee, 'cause women like me. I'm tall, dark and hansome and you third world ugly.
> *Lee*: I am not third world ugly, women think I'm cute. Like Snoopy.
> *James Carter*: Man, Snoopy is six inches taller than you.

BRAINSTORMERS

1. One of the characters in your film is an Australian and wants to refer to someone as a lay-about who never does any serious work. By referring to *www.spraakservice.net/slangportal*, what slang expression would best fit this description? What if the character were English? How about American?

2. Let's say you are going to use short subtitles in your movie but want to write the character's dialogue in the native language. By referring to *http://babelfish.altavista.com/translate.dyn*, how would your character say "I love you" in Spanish? In French? In German?

3. If you are writing a film with dialects, what resources would you employ to ensure that your wording and slang expressions are accurate and currently in use?

EVERY STORY NEEDS A POINT OF VIEW

In the preceding chapters, you've learned that each of your characters has something vital to say and that each has a different way of expressing it based on his or her age, education, ethnicity, social status and proximity to events. Even the *absence* of dialogue can speak volumes, summoning to mind the Chinese proverb, "Just because you have silenced a man does not mean that he has been conquered." Context, subtext, environmental visuals and body language all go into the mix of understanding what this story is really about and what we, as the viewers, are expected to learn from it.

With so many voices and opinions grappling for attention, sooner or later you're going to have to determine which one of them gets the spotlight. Whether you're writing a movie, a play or a novel, your audience needs to know from the outset whose point of view best reflects the film's theme and, thus, was chosen to relate the events to us. Accordingly, this will suggest who are the good guys, who are the bad guys, and who are the undecideds. This awareness then colors our interpretation of the events themselves.

In a tightly written screenplay, the designated point of view should be obvious in the first ten pages. In a 120-page script, this represents less than 10% of the movie. This formula can be used in any length project. For example, in a fifteen-minute/fifteen-page short, we need to know in less than a page and a half intro which character is our storyteller.

Obviously, a shift in point of view impacts our judgment of the facts. Apply this to day-to-day life. A valuable lamp gets broken at your house. There's your story, there's your little sister's story, there's your best bud's story. Which version is the truth?

LOOK & LEARN

Reversal of Fortune is based on the true life account of Sunny von Bulow, a wealthy heiress whose life may or may not have been compromised by her husband Claus. As you watch this film, identify whose point of view is governing the story. Is it Claus? Is it Alan Dershowitz, who has been hired by Claus to defend him against charges of attempted murder? Or is it Sunny herself who, as of this writing, remains in a coma induced by insulin in 1980?

Contingent on which viewpoint you choose, do you believe that Sunny's misfortune was a product of attempted homicide or suicide?

BRAINSTORMERS

1. Everyone knows the story of *Little Red Riding Hood.* What we know, however, is told from the third-party perspective of the writer. What if it were told to us in the first-party viewpoint of Red Riding Hood? What about the wolf? What about the grandmother? Last but not least, what about the woodsman? What unique view/biases would each one bring to this tale?

2. What is your favorite movie? Whose point of view governs this story? How would the story be told differently if assigned to a character other than this one? What aspects of the story could be explored that were previously untapped with the original point of view?

3. Which character's point of view will prevail in the film you want to write? Why do you feel this character is the best one to direct the course of the story? How would your story be different if told from the viewpoint of (1) the opposition or (2) a minor character?

FIRST ONE IN, LAST ONE OUT

Once you've decided whose point of view is going to prevail in your story, it's essential that you introduce him or her to the audience as fast as possible. If you don't, you run the risk of viewers initially bonding with your other characters and then wondering why they just dribble off into the woodwork, never to be seen again.

This often happens where writers start their story in the wrong place and dawdle to bring on the key player whose conflicts are meant to comprise the central plot. Let's say you're doing a film about a girl named Elizabeth. Her parents' names are Henry and Anne and the script starts out with Elizabeth's birth. Henry's not too keen about it; he really wanted a son instead. In fact, he's so vexed with Anne that he has her killed and marries somebody else. Baby Elizabeth, it seems, isn't going to take the stage until she's twenty-five and steps into her father's job. Even though your intention is to eventually show all the neat stuff she did after she became Queen of England, the slow, linear set-up mistakenly suggests that Henry is the one we're supposed to pay attention to. If Elizabeth is to "rule" in this script, she needs to be dominant from the get-go.

It's also important that whoever your star player is needs to either still be hanging around in the final frames or at least still be talked about by the other characters as having had an influence on their lives. What new screenwriters don't realize is that this bookend form of presence is an evaluation tool when studio readers, agents and consultants are swamped with scripts. Specifically, they will read the first ten pages and then the last five. Those in which the first in/last out rule has been followed will be read faster than those where the hero is undeclared at the opening and non-existent by FADE TO BLACK.

LOOK & LEARN

Otto Preminger's 1944 film-noir classic, *Laura*, offers an intriguing twist on the concept you've just learned. In this story, the title heroine has already been murdered in her apartment before the film begins. The detective who is investigating the case becomes as obsessed with her portrait as all of her adoring suitors were obsessed with Laura herself. Halfway into the film, the woman who has essentially been a backdrop ghost up until now suddenly walks in, very much alive.

Another film which cleverly establishes the pervasive influence of a deceased persona is the adaptation of Daphne Du Maurier's *Rebecca*. The new bride may be the designated storyteller in both the novel and the movie but it's her beautiful and mysterious predecessor around whom all events and interpersonal relationships revolve.

BRAINSTORMERS

1. Who's your favorite historical figure? What do you feel is the most significant thing about his/her life? If you were going to write a movie about this person, where would you start the plot to immediately hook an audience?

2. In *Seabiscuit*, how long does it take for the title character (the horse) and Red Pollard (the jockey) to show up in the storyline? If you were rewriting the script, how much of the expositional background would you trim?

3. Identify three films in which the villain is introduced to the audience prior to the hero. (Example: *The Devil's Own*.) Do you think this is a more effective device than showing us who the hero is first? Why or why not? Do you feel that a longer association time contributes to making a villain the more watchable and/or compelling character compared to a protagonist?

TREATMENTS

Somewhere between prose and script is a fusion called a film "treatment." Longer and more detailed in its scope than a synopsis, the purpose of the treatment is to walk a reader through the entire foundation of the story without including lines of dialogue. This can be compared to looking at the blueprint for a house as opposed to looking at the actual house itself. We know that it's going to be painted and have carpet, curtains, fixtures and furniture when it's done but, for the time being, we just want to be able to tell at a glance whether it's Victorian or ranch-style, how many levels it has, where the doors are, and the number of occupants it can accommodate.

Whether a treatment is drafted at the beginning of the project as a working outline for the writer or is developed after-the-fact as a marketing tool for pitching to producers, it is always written in present tense, introduces the key players, and reveals major plot points from start to finish. In addition, the treatment serves as a writing sample which demonstrates the author's knowledge of story structure and the ability to tie all of the elements together in an entertaining and cohesive fashion.

Without the writer having to think of all the words that will be coming out of the characters' mouths, a treatment can spend more time exploring what's going on in their heads that compels them to take action in response to the main conflict. The treatment-as-blueprint concept also lets you "erase" those occasions when you discover you've got a door that opens into a brick wall. It's much easier to fix these faux pas on the drafting table than halfway through construction of the full project! Treatments typically range from three to thirty pages depending on the length and complexity of the film itself.

LOOK & LEARN

A great online resource for learning to write treatments can be found at the Movie Spoiler website (*www.themoviespoiler.com*). These are detailed summaries of new (as well as classic) releases. The only differences are that (1) an unproduced script won't have the names of actors playing the roles; (2) the first introduction of a character in the story will be in capital letters; and (3) it won't include parenthetical remarks by the writer (e.g., "this will be important later" or "this scene is confusing but I think it's supposed to mean she still loves him"). The Movie Spoiler's webmaster also has a companion site for books (*www.thebookspoiler.com*) that follows the same present tense format. And, of course, there's also the longstanding CliffsNotes series (*www.cliffs.com*) which distills literature, poetry, drama and essays to a byte-size portion.

BRAINSTORMERS

1. The webmaster for The Movie Spoiler enthusiastically welcomes submissions by true movie hounds. Want to see your spoiler in print? Check back each week to see which spoilers are needed and submit one of your own following the format of existing submissions. In fact, that's your first assignment for this chapter.

2. What is the most recent sitcom or TV drama you have watched? To the best of your memory (or videotape!), write a two-page treatment of that episode. Remember to keep it in present tense and cover all significant plot points.

3. You've been asked to develop a new daytime soap opera. Write a five-page treatment for the pilot episode which introduces the recurring characters, their relationships to one another, and the first conflict that sets everything into play. Unlike a stand-alone film, end this one with a startling cliffhanger.

SPLAT! HITTING THE WALL WITH WRITER'S BLOCK

Writer's block (n.) a temporary inability to proceed with the composition of a novel, play, etc.

The bad news is that this malady isn't confined to beginners. Even people who have been writing for eons can suddenly be struck with a mental paralysis that causes their heads to go as blank as an empty computer screen. The good news is that the operative word is "temporary," easily curable by engaging in creative exercises to get the juices flowing again. Bookmark this chapter for whenever your brain gets stuck.

- If you could change anything about yourself (age, looks, status), what would it be? You wake up tomorrow and your wish has come true. Write a one-page diary entry about your first day as the "new you." Would you keep this wish or revert to the past? Why?

- Your hometown is giving you an award. What is it and what did you do to earn it? Prepare your answer as you'd like it to appear in a magazine interview.

- In order of importance, list the ten best things that have ever happened to you.

- If you were going to be marooned on an island for one month, what three items from your room would you take with you and why?

- Spin a globe, close your eyes and drop your finger on any spot to stop it. You are going to be a foreign exchange student in this place for one year. Write an essay about what you are most — and least — looking forward to in this experience.

- If you could spend an hour with anyone in history, who would it be and what would you most want to ask him or her?

- Write an eight-line rhyming poem about your favorite sport.

- Ten years ago, someone gave you a small, locked box and told you not to open it until now. (1) What is in the box and (2) why did they make you wait a decade?

- Rewrite Cinderella set in 1943 where the ball is at the USO.

- Describe your most recent dream/nightmare and what you think it means.

- If you could have a different set of parents, who would they be and why would you choose them?
- If you had three wishes, what would they be and why?
- What are you the most afraid of? Write 100 words about your greatest fear.
- You have the power and influence to enact a new state law. What would it be and why?
- You have only twenty-four hours left to live … in prison. What would your last meal be?
- Turn on the radio. Whatever song is playing is the score for your next film. What is the storyline and in what scene does this specific song first appear?

LOOK & LEARN

You're under a tight deadline. You have actors waiting breathlessly in the wings of a theater for you to write lines for them to come on stage and perform. Your production company is going to be closed if you don't come up with something clever by the next performance date. Such is the pressure for a tortured young William Shakespeare as portrayed by Joseph Fiennes in *Shakespeare in Love*. Fortunately, he has a lovely muse in the form of Gwyneth Paltrow to inspire him.

Compare and contrast this film and its elements to *Alex and Emma* in which a novelist must complete a new book in thirty days or risk ugly retaliation by the mob. Which of these two writers had the easier job?

BRAINSTORMERS

1. Who is your favorite film hero? Who is your favorite film villain? The two of them have decided that they want you to write a plot that they can act in together. What would that plot be? Which one of them would emerge the victor?
2. Write a 200-word letter in which you earnestly explain to your parents why you are dropping out of school to become an actor, a musician or an artist. Create a fictional persona who has just penned this same letter to his/her parents. If this were a feature film, what would the outcome be?
3. Go to an art gallery and study all the paintings. If you could spend a single afternoon in any one of them and actively interact with the subject matter, which painting would it be? What do you feel your choice says about your personality? Write a 100-word synopsis of a fantasy plot in which your lead character enters the same painting you picked. Would he or she choose to remain in the painting forever or return to real life?

GENRES ARE TO FILM WHAT MENUS ARE TO RESTAURANTS

What's your favorite kind of food? If your answer is Chinese, you probably wouldn't go to a Tex-Mex restaurant and find chow mein and eggs rolls prominently displayed on its menu. Nor would you expect to find New York–style hot dogs if you went into an establishment whose specialty was advertised as English tea and scones.

A correlation can be made to the ingredients found in different kinds of films. While there are plenty of movies that have "a little of this" and "a smidge of that," most of them concentrate on one specific flavor that they prepare especially well. This is called "genre" and it refers to the style or type of story that is being served up to a viewing public that's hungry for good entertainment.

Genre is also what makes it easy for you to find your favorite type of movie rental at the video store. If the selections were all mixed together like goulash, it could take you forever to find the latest martial arts film or family comedy. Instead, these works are neatly categorized according to their primary content. As you'll discover in the upcoming chapters, there are a number of basic genres (like beef, chicken and fish) and, within these divisions, subgenres (think of these as the compatible side dishes).

This is important to remember as you start developing your script because, unlike an online store where items can be virtually located in multiple sections, a traditional video/DVD outlet simply isn't going to have the shelf-space to cross-file your film in every conceivable grouping. This is also a good place to warn you not to make up genres that don't exist, e.g., "a science fiction action-adventure romantic thriller mystery with comedic overtones." Stick to the basics and you — and your audience — can't go wrong.

LOOK & LEARN

Legendary and historical heroes have always figured prominently in movies. The genre in which they're depicted, however, is subject to each director's individual vision. Let's take Robin Hood, the bandit of Sherwood Forest. In 1938, Errol Flynn's swashbuckling presence in *The Adventures of Robin Hood* made the plot an action/adventure. In 1991, Kevin Costner turned *Robin Hood, Prince of Thieves* into a storyline that focused more on the romance with Maid Marian. Two years later, *Robin Hood: Men in Tights* did a comedy lampoon of the Costner version which incorporated such spoofed lines as:

Robin Hood: [*first meeting Blinkin the blind servant*] Blinkin!
Blinkin: Master Robin, Is that you?
Robin Hood: Yes.
Blinkin: What? Back from the Crusades?
Robin Hood: Yes.
Blinkin: And alive?
Robin Hood: [*pause*] Yes.

Can you think of other personas and plots that are depicted in multiple genres?

BRAINSTORMERS

1. What types of films do you enjoy the most — films that make you laugh, cry, think, cringe, reminisce, cheer or sing along? Explain your answer.

2. How much does your prior awareness of a story (plot, starring actors, reviews) influence your expectations of what that film will deliver in terms of entertainment value? Would you ever go to a film you knew absolutely nothing about? Why or why not?

3. How do you view your everyday world? Is it a sitcom, a soap opera, a mystery, a science experiment? How do these views influence the type of film you want to develop and the genre with which you feel the most comfortable as a writer?

THE PERILS OF GENRE ZEITGEIST

When I was a freshman in high school, I begged my parents to buy me some *Hullabaloo* go-go boots. "Say what?" you say. *Hullabaloo*, a vintage precursor to MTV, was a one-season music program that appealed to the national teen craze of wanting to be British. Why? Because the British not only brought us the Beatles but kicky little mini-skirts, the Twiggy "mod" look, Mary Quant cosmetics, and signing all your notes with "Luv." Go-go boots — worn by the program's female dancers — were short, white and zipped on the side. To a teen girl, they epitomized coolness. English accents optional.

Fashion trends, of course, tend to have a short shelf life. No sooner do you start imitating a new style than it's replaced by something else. The same thing occurs with movies. The current popularity of a genre is often a product of something called "Zeitgeist" — the mood and intellect of a collective culture. During the 1940s, for instance, audiences wanted escapist fare like comedies and musicals to take their minds off of the war years. A decade later, westerns ruled at the box office, attesting to the public's need to see good guys (Democracy) trouncing the threat of bad guys (Communism).

Within your own lifetime, you've probably seen this phenomenon in film themes whereby the overnight success of a certain storyline is rapidly followed by a succession of cheesy imitators. What these trends reveal is that whatever is "hot" this year is likely to be old news by the time you hop on board. The message, then, is threefold: (1) focus your energy on the genre you like best; (2) learn the rudiments of multiple genres to develop a diversified portfolio of spec scripts; or (3) develop classic themes that — like a pair of basic black pumps — can be matched to a variety of outfits (genres) better than *Hullabaloo* boots.

LOOK & LEARN

One of the best websites regarding teen-oriented movies made between the 1950s (the birth of teen films) and the present is *www.hollywoodteenmovies.com*. This site not only invites you to compare some of the teen heartthrobs of the past with stars of the twenty-first century but also look at some of the popular teen TV shows, movie quotes, cult classics and musicals. As far removed as some of the older scenarios and plots seem to be from our contemporary sense of Zeitgeist, they are united by the universal themes of transitioning from youth to adulthood, finding outlets of creative expression and individualism, and experiencing the first tentative tastes of freedom and responsibility.

BRAINSTORMERS

1. From the website listed above, select and watch any movie from the 1960s. Compare and contrast this to any teen-oriented film in the same genre from the present day. (Example: *The Love Bug* versus *Herbie, Fully Loaded*.) How have the attitudes and dreams of teens changed with the passage of four decades? How have they stayed the same?

2. *Happy Days* (which ran from 1974–1984) was a sitcom set in the 1950s. What themes did the producers utilize to bridge the time gap? What made this show popular with audience members who had not been teens themselves during the specific time period being represented?

3. What is your favorite teen-oriented weekly program? What does this program say or do in terms of reflecting the collective mindset of the country toward teenagers? How about the mindset of the world? How does its particular genre reinforce the series' underlying message?

GENRE DICTATES STRUCTURE

Moviegoers often pick a film based on their expectations of its speci-fied genre. If they want to laugh, they go to a comedy. If they want to scream, they go to a horror film. If they're taking someone special on a date, they'll probably pick a romance. While it's easy enough to rec-ognize what *elements* you need to put into your comedy, horror or romance script to satisfy a genre's requirements, determining *what happens when* is a lot more challenging. Structure — the physical order in which characters and actions are introduced — is a product of the genre chosen to communicate that particular story.

In a romance, for instance, the happily-ever-hopefuls need to equitably share screen-time, even if they're not in every scene together. In a murder mystery, a dead body needs to show up as early as possible. In a horror film, a ghoul's actions are witnessed long before we ever see the actual ghoul. In a fantasy, a legend usually sets the stage for action rather than being tacked on as an explanatory postscript in the final credits. In a comedy, the silliness keeps getting sillier as the characters get more frantic.

Storyboards or story cards (for non-artists) are an effective way of structuring your script before you start writing it. Here's how it works: Using a package of 3x5 index cards, write each character's name, each location and each significant event/action on a separate card. Lay the cards out so that the data on each one is visible. Then the fun starts! Rearrange them until you've established a sequence that is consistent with the expectations of that genre, introduces key players and conflicts early, and progressively escalates in energy. Refer to this sequence as you begin writing in order to stay focused on the physical organization which will hold your whole story together.

LOOK & LEARN

Have you ever watched your parent(s) prepare a meal? If you're having soup, a main course and dessert, you've probably noticed that the preparation and cooking of these courses doesn't all start at the same time. Not only do different types of food cook at different speeds but serving a meal out of order — even if you'd *like* to eat dessert first! — breaks the traditional rules of dining expectation. So, too, would it tweak convention if you had sweet and sour Chinese soup, Hungarian goulash and concluded with Mexican churros. Some cuisines — like subgenres — are compatible with one another; others are not. In a "hybrid" context, the respective rules of the integrated genres still apply in terms of introducing characters and conflicts. A good film that illustrates this is *Ghostbusters*, which melds comedy, horror and a splash of romance and introduces each genre's components in the same sequence as if it were *strictly* a comedy, horror or romance script.

BRAINSTORMERS

1. Draw three columns on a horizontal piece of paper and label them "Comedy, Horror, Romance." Down the left side, list Act 1, Act 2 and Act 3. Watch *Ghostbusters*. During each act, list each comedic element, horror scene and romantic moment as it occurs. When the film is over, study the sequence in each column to reinforce your understanding of genre's influence on script structure.

2. Make story cards for the film you want to write. Put a red dot on every card where your main character is present. Are there any long gaps that are dot-less? Remedy this by moving cards around or creating filler scenes featuring your hero.

3. Internet Movie Database (*www.imdb.com*) labels films by multiple genres. For *The Princess Bride*, identify the elements of each genre that is listed for it.

GENRE BLING-BLING

Back when I started my own theater company, I realized from the outset I'd be able to do something that would daunt other fledgling troupes. Specifically, I could write and produce plays that transpired in any historical period. The reason is that one of my best friends was a costume designer named Dick Crane whose entire third floor of his Victorian house was filled with vintage clothes, hats, footwear and bolts of fabric and accessories that allowed us to strut onstage in sartorial (and authentic) splendor. There were even times whereby his latest purchases dictated what I'd write next (e.g., "I just bought twenty yards of gold lamé on sale. Let's do a play about sultans.") Without Dick, the Hamlett Players would have been relegated to contemporary themes and trolling their own closets.

Fledgling film producers face similar challenges, often choosing new scripts on the basis of (1) what's the least amount of money I can make this for and (2) what will utilize the resources I already have access to. This is important to remember when you're choosing the best genre to convey your plot as it's always easier to add "glitz" later than to pen scripts that are reliant on lots of glitz and CGI just to deliver the heart of the story.

While you should always pick the genre for which you have the most affinity, recognize that period settings will almost always cost more than those set in the here and now. Also pricey are ones which involve dangerous stunts, car chases, large casts, animals and outdoor scenes that place a cast and crew at the mercy of the elements and fickle lighting. Interestingly, horror films tend to be the cheapest and invite the most creativity — no doubt an entrepreneurial by-product of Halloween memories and using such materials as ketchup, food coloring, cottage cheese and pasta to simulate all manner of squishy "guts."

LOOK & LEARN

In the summer of 1999, a scary film that cost a mere $35,000 turned an enormous profit of over $200 million. *The Blair Witch Project*, however, wasn't the first flick made on the cheap. *El Mariachi* ($7,000), *The Brothers McMullen* ($25,000) and *Clerks* ($27,000) each passed the million mark right out of the gate. At the opposite end of the spectrum are mega-budget films that not only recouped their investments but made nice profits as well: *Spider-Man 2*, *Titanic*, *Lord of the Rings: The Return of the King*, *Jurassic Park* and *Shrek 2*, to name a few. And, of course, there are the losers who spent far more than they earned: *Stealth* (lost $113,047,792), *The Adventures of Pluto Nash* (lost $96,452,503), *The Alamo* (lost $80,044,319), *Alexander* (lost $72,851,405). For more facts, visit *www.the-numbers.com/movies/records/budgets.html*. To learn about the budget process, add "How to Make a Movie for Under $800" to your screen books library.

BRAINSTORMERS

1. What are the most expensive elements in the film you'd like to write? Are they critical to the successful telling of the story? Explain in a 100-word essay.

2. If you were writing a story set in an earlier time period, what techniques would you use in the writing of your scenes, settings and characters to keep the overall budget as low as possible and attractive to a producer with limited funds?

3. Can this movie be saved? Go to the website listed above and select any movie with which you're familiar under "Biggest Money Losers Based on Absolute Loss on Worldwide Gross" or "Biggest Money Losers Based on Return on Investment." Explain in 100 words what you would have done to reduce the budget (including a change of cast or, where applicable, a change of genre or venue).

DON'T SWITCH GENRES IN MIDSTREAM

Whatever genre you decide your film is going to be, your audience is going to expect you to stay with it from start to finish. Let's return to the restaurant analogy to demonstrate why consistency is a crucial ingredient in delivering a satisfying story.

Chinese cuisine is typically served in a setting with colors, fixtures and artworks that reflect the Far East. The cooks and the servers are usually Asian and converse amongst themselves in their native language. The plates, bowls, cups and utensils (chopsticks and large, porcelain spoons) are what you would expect to find in a traditional Chinese dining room. If you listen closely, you might even hear Chinese music playing in the background. These combined elements contribute to an ambiance that allows you to forget for the next hour that you're in Fargo, North Dakota or that the noisy bustle of downtown Manhattan is just on the other side of the front door.

Now imagine that just as you're anticipating a plate of your favorite kung pao chicken, potstickers, sweet and sour pork and hot tea, someone cranks up the volume. It's no longer Chinese music you're hearing, however; it's Eminem. And what's this? Your server looks like Shrek but is dressed as a pirate. He has also taken the liberty of bringing you guacamole and nachos instead of potstickers. Try as you might to enjoy the meal you came in for, the distractions are going to keep you off-balance and confused.

This same thing occurs when a screenwriter either hasn't decided what kind of genre he or she wants for the film or gets bored midway through the story and starts to take the characters down a different path that just isn't compatible with the original destination.

LOOK & LEARN

On August 25, 1992, a new TV series debuted called *Covington Cross*. Set in medieval times, the plot was essentially *My Three Sons* (plus a daughter) in *Camelot*. Two of its stars — Nigel Terry and Cherie Lunghi — were already well versed in this genre, having acted together as King Arthur and Guenevere in *Excalibur*. Terry's affinity for the Dark Ages had been honed even earlier (1968) as Peter O'Toole and Katharine Hepburn's youngest son in *The Lion in Winter*.

Unfortunately, *Covington Cross* was not only encumbered by an unstable time slot (presidential candidate Ross Perot bought out one of its broadcasts for his ad campaign) but was plagued by the inability to decide if it was a comedy, a drama, a farce, a feminist first (the daughter was excellent on horseback and with swords), a romance or an action/adventure. The show squeaked to its final performance on October 31, 1992.

BRAINSTORMERS

1. Has your favorite TV show ever taken a strange turn that compromised its original appeal? What was the show and what would you have done differently to keep it watchable? (This self-destructive phenomenon, by the way, has been coined "Jumping the Shark." Read more about it at *www.jumptheshark.com*.)

2. Which genre do you think is harder for a writer to stay on message — a comedy or a drama? Explain your answer.

3. If an audience knew nothing about your story before they came in to watch it, how far into the film would it take before they knew what kind of movie (genre) you had written?

A COMEDY IS SOMETHING THAT MAKES US LAUGH

Audiences have been laughing at onscreen antics ever since the first Lumière film — a short — flickered to life in the 1890s. Because early filmmakers had yet to figure out how to attach sound to their moving pictures, comedy was initially confined to physical humor such as pratfalls, food fights, silly stunts and wacky chase scenes. By the 1930s, such sight gags began to be replaced by snappy repartee and the emergence of comedic teams like the Marx Brothers, the Three Stooges, and duos such as Stan Laurel/Oliver Hardy and Bud Abbott/Lou Costello. Movies today have expanded the definition of comedy to include star-crossed romance, parodies/spoofs of other genres and prior films, fish out of water (remember our chapter on extraordinary and ordinary?) and dramedies (comedies that incorporate dark or unconventional themes).

As broad a genre as comedy encompasses, however, it's also the most subjective in terms of audience response. The reason is that an appreciation of things that are funny is based on more factors than just the lines and visuals. A writer has to take into account the viewer's age, gender, ethnicity, IQ, and his or her frame of reference to the subject matter itself. How many times, for instance, have you come home from school with what you thought was a rip-snorting knee-slapper about Kenny Oglethorpe dropping his algebra book on Missy Purdue's egg salad sandwich and the gross sound it made when it squished? Pretty funny stuff. Then again, I guess you had to be there.

Humor is also interpreted differently across diverse cultures. Even in the United Kingdom, the fact that everyone speaks English doesn't translate to automatic enjoyment of American jokes, slang or allusions to contemporary pop culture.

LOOK & LEARN

The following films provide good study examples of some of comedy's sub-genres.

- Parodies and Spoofs: *Spaceballs, Young Frankenstein, Blazing Saddles, Not Another Teen Movie, Robin Hood: Men in Tights*

- Romantic Comedy: *While You Were Sleeping, Alex and Emma, When Harry Met Sally, Sleepless in Seattle, Bridget Jones' Diary, A Lot Like Love*

- Fish Out of Water: *Big, 13 Going on 30, Dave, Moon Over Parador, The Inspector General, Freaky Friday*

- Dramedies/Black Humor: *Harold and Maude, Fight Club, Lemony Snicket's A Series of Unfortunate Events, Bad Santa, Being There*

- Slapstick: *Animal Crackers, Duck Soup,* The *Bellboy, Abbott and Costello Meet Frankenstein, There's Something About Mary, Who's That Girl?*

BRAINSTORMERS

1. What kind of movies make you laugh? Make a list of the ten funniest films you have ever seen. What elements do these ten movies have in common?

2. Ask the following people to tell you what they think are the ten funniest films they've ever seen: (1) a parent; (2) a grandparent; (3) your best friend; (4) a family member who is younger than you are; (5) a sports coach; and (6) someone who is originally from another country. How do their replies compare to yours? What do you think accounts for these differences in opinion? How will you apply these observations to your own comedic stories?

3. Which movies does Hollywood think are the best comedies? See for yourself at *www.afi.com*. On the right hand side of the screen, click on "AFI's 100 Year Series" which will then take you to their list of "100 Laughs." How many of the films that were named in Questions #1 and #2 are on AFI's list?

A DRAMA IS SOMETHING THAT MAKES US SAD, MAD, DISTURBED OR CONTEMPLATIVE

The opposite of something that's funny is something that's serious. Dramas — just like their comedic counterparts — can take place in any setting or century and can be about fictional characters, historical figures or those who are a representative mix of individuals who might have witnessed or participated in a particular event (e.g., a fictitious soldier interacting with General Robert E. Lee or a student deciding whether he should join his peers in the protests at China's Tiananmen Square). Dramatic works are also often inspired by newspaper and magazine articles or by journals of people who have survived harrowing tragedies, triumphed against the odds, or gone through coming-of-age angst in the uncertain journey to adulthood.

Unlike comedies, dramas are not as reliant on such factors as age and IQ in order to make a point with their audience. The reason is that they not only have the capacity to strike a common emotional chord — most everyone can relate to feelings of sadness, confusion and anger — but they explore subjects that are of recurring concern to society at large, e.g., racism, crime, juvenile delinquency, poverty, violence, political corruption, drug and alcohol abuse, sex and mental illness.

While comedies allow some latitude for characters to show their best and worst sides in contrived situations, a drama goes much further, forcing its players not only to square off against external demons but to confront the fears, flaws, guilt trips and prejudices that reside within their own psyches. This vicarious realism then becomes a catalyst for viewers to look deeper within themselves and the world around them.

LOOK & LEARN

The following films provide good study samples of some of drama's sub-genres.

- Intrigue: *All the President's Men, The Manchurian Candidate, JFK, Mr. Smith Goes to Washington, The Interpreter*

- Mental Illness: *A Beautiful Mind, One Flew Over the Cuckoo's Nest, Frances, The Aviator*

- Prejudice: *Do the Right Thing, Philadelphia, In the Heat of the Night, Yentl, Men of Honor, Schindler's List*

- Troubled Families: *Ordinary People, Kramer vs. Kramer, Lost in Yonkers, American Beauty, Finding Neverland, The Hours*

- In the Courtroom: *The Verdict, A Few Good Men, To Kill a Mockingbird*

- Sports: *Brian's Song, Million Dollar Baby, Radio, Seabiscuit, Rocky*

BRAINSTORMERS

1. Flip through today's newspaper and find three current stories that you think would make a good dramatic movie. Who are the primary characters in each one? What is the tragedy, social issue or injustice that has occurred which would lend itself to a dramatic theme? Is the central conflict of sufficient substance that it would make a good feature film or is it better suited to a short? Explain your answer.

2. What is the saddest, most upsetting or most moving thing that you have ever experienced? In a 100-word essay, explain how this particular event changed your emotional outlook on life or toward the people around you.

3. Choose one of the following scenarios: a wedding, a birthday party, a bar mitzvah, a graduation, a funeral, a reunion, an anniversary, a bridal shower, a homecoming, a birth. Something dramatic and unexpected is about to go wrong which will impact the lives of everyone in attendance. What is this event and how will it bring out the best and worst in these characters? How will the story be resolved?

A SCI-FI FILM TAKES US OUT OF THIS WORLD

Science fiction and fantasy are often lumped together into the same category. This is owing to the fact that both genres flirt with mystical notions of "what might have been" and futuristic projections of "what could be." For the purposes of this book, the two genres will be treated separately yet offered with the understanding that, in the context of some projects, the line is blurred to the point of crossover.

Does technology sometimes make you nervous? Do you gaze at the stars and ever wonder if extraterrestrials are gazing back? Filmmakers as early as the 1920s recognized that fears of progress run amok and anxieties about outer space predators made great fodder for movies, especially given the already popular following of these themes in comic strips. Intergalactic heroes Buck Rogers and Flash Gordon — armed with spiffy ray guns and navigating mysterious spaceships — quickly became mainstays of the Saturday matinee. Because real space travel was not yet a reality, this escapist fare gave producers a chance to pull out all the stops in creating imaginatively quirky realms inhabited by alien monsters, evil despots with names like Ming the Merciless, and damsels in distress whose makeup and hairstyles uncannily matched their counterparts on Earth.

The national paranoia of the 1950s — triggered by the Cold War — was mirrored in an abundance of films about space invaders, radioactive mutants, defrosted dinosaurs and mad scientists seeking to control their victims' minds. Such themes, of course, were all a metaphor for the threat of Communism. Interestingly, sci-fi films and westerns both hit a box-office high during this period, reinforcing the message that — no matter the turf — good guys will always win.

LOOK & LEARN

While you're waiting for the next Trekkie convention to come to town, these selections will demonstrate the diversity of the sci-fi genre.

- Aliens Among Us: *It Came from Outer Space, Invaders from Mars, Close Encounters of the Third Kind, Alien, War of the Worlds*

- Prehistoric Predators: *The Lost World, Jurassic Park, Attack of the Crab Monsters* (Trivia note: The Professor from Gilligan's Island was a professor in this last one, too.)

- Radioactive Plots: *Attack of the 50-Foot Woman, Fantastic Four, The Fifth Element, X the Unknown, Them!*

- Clones and Computers Run Amok: *Invasion of the Body Snatchers, 2001: A Space Odyssey* (Trivia note: The onboard computer is HAL; move each letter ahead by one and it actually spells IBM), *Minority Report*

- Space Sagas: *Star Trek, Star Wars, Battlestar Gallactica, Andromeda*

BRAINSTORMERS

1. It was only 1968 in Earth years but 3978 A.D. when a crew of astronauts led by Charlton Heston found themselves on a distant planet ruled by a bunch of militaristic apes. The punch line, of course, is that the mystery planet wasn't quite as distant as the Earthlings imagined. Identify three sci-fi movies (or *Twilight Zone* sci-fi episodes) in which you were surprised by a twist ending.

2. Take any non sci-fi movie you have seen and explain how you would adapt it to make it a sci-fi story. Be sure to include a description of the setting, the new names of the characters, any special talents or powers your characters possess, and how the plot would be resolved.

3. Many TV shows have depicted extraterrestrials trying to fit into a normal Earth life (*My Favorite Martian, Mork and Mindy, ALF, Third Rock from the Sun*). Write a short story in which an Earthling has to adjust to daily life with a suburban family in another galaxy.

A WESTERN FILM IS ALWAYS ABOUT A SHOWDOWN

The Great Train Robbery is a twelve-minute short that was shot in various wooded parks throughout New Jersey and debuted in 1903. Audiences have been in love with this genre ever since, drawn to the mystique of cowboys, bandits, dancehall girls and those inevitable dare words, "This town ain't big enough for the two of us."

This era — perhaps more than any other — represents the American counterpart to England's Knights of the Round Table. Rugged heroes, virtuous schoolmarms, sage geezers, plucky townsfolk and, of course, trusty steeds have the added advantage of being based on or inspired by the exploits of real men and women who peopled the burgeoning landscape west of the Mississippi during the years immediately following the Civil War. A man and his gun could go far. A director and his camera could go even farther.

Is it any wonder that during the 1950s, film directors were wildly enthusiastic to bring this brand of adventure to movie screens throughout the country and to offer viewers a respite from the pervasive anxieties about Communism, racism, and whether aliens in outer space were plotting a sneak attack? During 1954 alone, one out of every five films was about a man and his horse and a slow ride into the sunset.

It may also interest you to know that after his famous gunfight at the O.K. Corral, Wyatt Earp himself developed quite an interest in this newfangled thing called "talking pictures" and offered his services as a professional consultant to filmmakers who wanted to capture what the rough and tumble Wild West was really like. Earp not only lived until the age of eighty (it was 1929 by then) but had cowboy actor pals William S. Hart and Tom Mix as his pallbearers.

LOOK & LEARN

Looking for some vicarious excitement set in the days of the Wild West? Here are some top picks to get you started, partner.

- *Butch Cassidy and the Sundance Kid*
- *High Noon*
- *The Magnificent Seven*
- *Tombstone*
- *Rio Bravo*
- *Shane*
- *The Good, the Bad and the Ugly*
- *Pale Rider*
- *The Searchers*
- *The Man Who Shot Liberty Valance*
- *Cheyenne Autumn*
- *Dances with Wolves*

BRAINSTORMERS

1. In *Tombstone*, Kurt Russell and Val Kilmer respectively play Wyatt Earp and Doc Holliday. Compare and contrast this gun-toting duo's personalities and approach to justice with the modern crime-fighting pair of Roger Murtaugh and Martin Riggs (played by Danny Glover and Mel Gibson) in *Lethal Weapon*.

2. Take any non-Western film you like and explain how you would adapt the characters and plot to the Old West. Oh, and write the lyrics for what will be the film's theme song when you're finished.

3. Buffalo Bill Cody has been portrayed on screen more than any other western hero. Pretend you're a talk show host who has just booked the real Buffalo Bill Cody. Come up with ten questions you'd like this legendary figure to answer on the show. How might you use his answers to develop and write an interesting movie?

A FANTASY FILM IS A TICKET TO ALL THINGS MAGICAL

Swords and sorcery. Wizards and talking animals. Time travel and parallel universes. If stories involving elements of magic have you under their spell, you may want to consider writing a script for the fantasy genre. "Magic" — as opposed to science and technology — is the operative word here, even though a number of space-age adventures such as *Star Wars* conjure eye-popping special effects that would seem to fit a fantasy definition. The origins of such high-tech phenomena, however, can be traced along a path of human invention. Enchantment, on the other hand, is an embodiment of legend, mysticism, reincarnation and faith whose existence has no logical explanation.

It's no small coincidence that the teens and tweens of my generation connected with J. R. R. Tolkien's world of Hobbits as enthusiastically as your own generation has made J. K. Rowling's Hogwarts a household word. When you stop to consider how many people are first introduced to reading through stories that begin "Once upon a time…" it's easy to understand the universal fascination with fairy tale settings, inexplicable events, and bewitched characters that so effortlessly lift us out of the ordinariness of everyday life, chores and algebra homework.

What's crucial in crafting a great fantasy, however, is to remember that even in a realm that's governed entirely by magic, the emotions that govern the hearts of good guys (*and* bad) are based on a purely mortal code of right and wrong. Whether he's casting spells or dispatching dragons, he's still going to worry if the new girl likes him and whether he really has the wits to outsmart a giant. And in the end, he wants nothing less than the rest of us — a happily ever after that is achieved on the basis of faith and well grounded merits.

LOOK & LEARN

Looking for elements of fantasy? The following films are excellent prospects. Keep in mind, of course, that several of them also fold in a liberal dose of romance, humor and happily ever after.

- Medieval Machinations: *Dragonheart, Ladyhawke, Excalibur, The Princess Bride*

- Time Travel: *Somewhere in Time, Highlander*

- Myth and Magic: *Jason and the Argonauts, Conan the Barbarian, The Lord of the Rings* trilogy, *Jumanji*

- Contemporary Wizards: *Harry Potter* series, *Bewitched, I Dream of Jeannie, Charmed, Sabrina the Teenage Witch*

- Say It with Song: *Beauty and the Beast, Aladdin, The Wizard of Oz*

- Divine Guidance & Reincarnation: *Oh, God!, You Never Can Tell, All Dogs Go to Heaven, It's a Wonderful Life, Heaven Can Wait*

BRAINSTORMERS

1. Movies based on comic book superheroes used to be categorized as fantasy. Today, they are of sufficient number to be in a class by themselves. In a 100-word essay, identify your favorite superhero and explain why his or her background and special powers lend themselves well to the medium of film.

2. Based on your understanding of the dynamics of ordinary and extraordinary individuals and situations, which do you think is more difficult to sustain in a script: a mortal having to cope with an enchanted realm or a person with magical powers who has to function in a world of normal humans?

3. Time travel is a popular subgenre of fantasy. If your character had the magical power to go backward or forward in time, would it be harder for him or her to live without modern conveniences and yet have knowledge of events to come or to take a peek at future technology and yet possess no insider knowledge of how any of it works?

A HORROR FILM WILL MAKE YOU SLEEP WITH THE LIGHTS ON

Vampires and zombies and ghouls — oh my! Why is it that scary beasts and things that go bump in the night are so popular with audiences? Psychologists have determined that horror films are a safe way to get the adrenalin pumping without actually putting oneself in the same room or on the same dark road with anything bloodthirsty and malevolent. Whether the objects of terror are supernatural predators, vengeful ghosts, man-made monsters or psycho freaks in hockey masks, horror films share the common denominator of reminding us of our most primal fears.

While recent films invoke terror through graphic death/dismemberment scenes involving gallons of blood, guts, and brains ("slasher" flicks), earlier works in this genre relied more on the audience's own power of imagination to fill in the frightening blanks. To this end, characters were often seen opening a door inside a haunted house and reacting with a scream and facial expression so contorted with fright that obviously whatever they were looking at was horrible beyond words. Another interesting transition from past to present has been less emphasis on fog-shrouded cemeteries and creepy Celtic castles and more leanings toward modern suburbia. One needs only to study the works of horror master Stephen King, of course, to recognize that even the most harmless looking facades and inanimate objects can secretly harbor and unleash Satanic forces.

Many horror plots derive from regional folklore and campfire ghost stories. There is even a body of contemporary material you may have heard of called "Urban Legends." Examples of these tall tales can be found on such sites as *www.snopes.com*, *www.urban legends.about.com*, and *www.urbanlegendsonline.com*.

LOOK & LEARN

Lon Chaney. Boris Karloff. Vincent Price. Bela Lugosi. Each of these legendary actors became famous for portraying characters you'd never want to pick to be your roommate. In addition to looking up their most celebrated roles at the Internet Movie Data Base (*www.imdb.com*), here are some other top picks for your self-study fright night at the movies:

- *The Shining*
- *The Omen*
- *The Blair Witch Project*
- *Psycho*
- *Rosemary's Baby*
- *The Exorcist*
- *Jason*
- *A Nightmare on Elm Street*
- *The Texas Chainsaw Massacre*
- *Dracula*
- *Frankenstein*
- *The Wolf Man*
- *Dr. Jekyll & Mr. Hyde*
- *Secret Window*
- *Jeepers-Creepers*
- *Scream*

BRAINSTORMERS

1. Choose one of the urban legends from a website listed on the previous page and describe how you would turn it into a ten-minute horror film. How many characters would you use? What would the setting be? Do you plan to scare your audience through actual visuals or utilize the power of suggestion?

2. You are on the committee for this year's Haunted House. Your assignment is the parlor — the very first room that Halloween visitors will enter. Describe what you would do to stage a bone-chiller introduction for them that they'll never forget.

3. What is the scariest movie you have ever seen? What elements in this film terrified you the most? Did these fears have any relationship to actual experiences you've had (e.g., you were once bitten by a wild dog and this film had a wild dog in it)?

A ROMANCE IS A PAS DE DEUX

In ballet, the French phrase above refers to a "dance for two." In film, this dance is a mating ritual that is fraught with misunderstandings, missteps and misguided intentions — all of which are orchestrated by the writer to bring two characters together for what we hope will be a happily ever after.

Romance knows no bounds of century or geography, nor is every cinematic courtship automatically destined for the altar. In some love stories, the characters are *already* a couple when we first meet them and yet are struggling with the question of whether they should remain so or drift apart into separate orbits. In other plots, the bond of affection is threatened by forces outside of their personal control — a call to serve one's country, an onset of financial challenges, disapproval by domineering or prejudicial family members, or a grim prognosis impacting the life of one of the partners. The romance genre is also replete with evidence that combustible opposites will always attract and that the line that exists between love and hate can magically be erased with a single kiss.

While romances are typically peopled with a lot of supporting players — parents, co-workers, best friends and even rivals — it's important that none of these individuals or their own emotional baggage overshadow the central relationship at stake. Screenwriters need to remember that neither half of the star-crossed duo should disappear from the pages for long stretches at a time. Even if the guy and gal aren't in every scene together (and *Sleepless in Seattle* is a great example of this), the idea of romance should never stray far from their minds or the minds of the audience.

LOOK & LEARN

You never know where Cupid's arrow is going to strike next and these films are no exception to illustrating that cosmic mystery:

- *You've Got Mail*
- *Somewhere in Time*
- *Say Anything*
- *Here on Earth*
- *Shakespeare in Love*
- *Before Sunrise*
- *The Way We Were*
- *Casablanca*
- *The American President*
- *10 Things I Hate About You*
- *Moonstruck*
- *Bride and Prejudice*
- *The Sure Thing*
- *Doctor Zhivago*

What movies does the American Film Institute think are the most memorably romantic? Check out the 100 Best Passions list at *www.afi.com*. And while you're at it, count how many of them *don't* end up as "happily ever afters."

BRAINSTORMERS

1. Have you ever wished that you could play matchmaker with some of the lonely hearts who place ads in the classifieds? Now is your chance. Select two ads from today's newspaper and describe the setting in which they meet for their first date. Were both of them honest in their self-descriptions and interests? How does this impact the other party's reaction to them upon actually meeting?

2. Is it better to have loved and lost than never to have loved at all? Provide your answer to this question in a 100-word essay.

3. Who do you think is the most romantic actor of all time? Who do you think is the most romantic actress of all time? If you were able to use both of these romantic actors in a film, what would the storyline be and what kind of characters would the two of them play?

A THRILLER KEEPS YOU GUESSING FROM START TO FINISH

The words "thriller" and "suspense" are often used interchangeably to describe plots which zigzag from one menacing surprise to the next. Usually at the center of all of this intrigue is a protagonist who unwittingly stumbles upon a shocking secret, witnesses an assassination, or gets involved with some sort of risky escape or dangerous mission for which he or she possesses no matching skills. Murder mysteries are a popular off-shoot of this genre, as are dark plots involving medical malpractice, political corruption, high-tech spies and manipulation of courtroom jurors. There is also a substantive crossover into genres such as sci-fi and horror in which a state of paranoia is induced for the characters (and audience) by shadowy alien predators and slick psycho stalkers.

One of the masters of putting innocent bystanders into nail-biting jeopardy was Alfred Hitchcock. His fascination with the shady and/or twisted side of human character is reflected in such works as *Vertigo*, *Lifeboat*, *Dial M for Murder*, *Strangers on a Train* and *Psycho*. This was also a man who made everyone look at crows and seagulls with a wary eye after the release of *The Birds*, a chilling film in which a seaside community on the northern California coast falls prey to an inexplicable airborne attack. Any of Hitchcock's films are great study material for understanding the thriller genre.

Truly riveting stories, of course, derive from subjects close to home; specifically, those that reside under the same roof. In *The Bad Seed*, a perfect little daughter is actually a perfectly cold-blood killer. In *Sleeping with the Enemy*, a wife has to fake her own death to escape an abusive husband. And in *Rebecca*, the new Mrs. DeWinter discovers that adjusting to life at Manderlay might call for a change of household staff.

LOOK & LEARN

In 2001, the American Film Institute released its list of the 100 most thrilling films.* Among those you'll find at *www.afi.com* are:

- *The Silence of the Lambs*
- *Double Indemnity*
- *Fatal Attraction*
- *Marathon Man*
- *Cape Fear*
- *Laura*
- *12 Angry Men*
- *What Ever Happened to Baby Jane?*
- *The Manchurian Candidate*
- *North by Northwest*

*Many of these are combined with elements of sci-fi, horror, and action/adventure.

BRAINSTORMERS

1. What is the most thrilling or suspenseful movie you have ever seen? What creative devices were used to keep you guessing about the outcome of the story?

2. Your new next-door neighbor is a nice enough person who always seems to invite a lot of people over. The curious thing, though, is that during the past month you have never seen any of them actually *leave*. He has now invited your parents to dinner at the end of the week. How would you go about finding out what's going on? And what exactly *is* going on?

3. In *The Bourne Identity*, a man discovers that he has no memory but lots of money, lots of specialized skills … and lots of enemies. If you were this character, how would you go about discovering your identity before the bad guys can discover your whereabouts? (And did we also mention that you only have twenty-four hours to accomplish this?)

ACTION/ADVENTURE FILMS ARE AN "E" TICKET TO FUN

Once upon a time in a place called Disneyland, access to the various rides was traded for coupons torn from a little book and ranging in value from "A" to "E." To a kid (and yes, most adults as well), "E" tickets were as good as gold, granting the bearer admittance to magical realms that were far removed from the park's Anaheim surroundings. An "E" ticket could take you into the jungles of Africa, propel you into the farthest reaches of space, or splash you into the midst of pirates plundering an 1800s Louisiana seaport. For whatever the duration of a ride, an "E" ticket offered the ultimate escape from reality (unlike a swirling teacup "A" ticket which only left you feeling nauseous).

Action and adventure films provide that same kind of vicarious rush. Often set in exotic locales and featuring non-stop chases, explosions, martial arts, poisonous snakes and death-defying rescues from impossible circumstances, the villains and heroes of these two genres are purely bad and good and battling one another for control of a treasure, control of the world or control of Mother Nature. Many of them, in fact, could easily transition to the pages of comic strips without losing any substance. And while romance can certainly play a part in the adrenalin-laced equation, it's never at the expense of saving the universe or discovering where the Knights Templar stashed their cache of antiquities.

With the exception of their flirtations with danger and their stubbornness to stay focused on a quest — no matter how harrowing — the heroes and heroines of these films are the kind of men and women that audience members themselves would most like to be… in their dreams.

LOOK & LEARN

Romance writer Joan Wilder's life soon starts to imitate that of her plucky heroines when her sister is kidnapped by Colombian thugs and she has no choice but to try to rescue her. *Romancing the Stone* is one of many action/adventure films that keeps the excitement in high gear.

Here are some more you'll enjoy learning from:

- *Raiders of the Lost Ark*
- *Spy Kids*
- *The African Queen*
- *The Crimson Pirate*
- *Mission Impossible*
- *The Perfect Storm*
- *National Treasure*
- *Shanghai Knights*
- *The Mummy*
- *The Adventures of Robin Hood*
- *La Femme Nikita*
- *Lara Croft, Tomb Raider*
- *Master and Commander: The Far Side of the World*
- *Charlie's Angels*

And, of course, anything with the inimitable and suave James Bond (no matter which Bond actor you prefer) fits this list, too.

BRAINSTORMERS

1. Why do the personalities of action/adventure heroes lend themselves so well to serialization? Explain your answer in a 100-word essay.

2. Do you think that it's easier to write an action/adventure story that is set in the past, the present or the future? Explain your answer. Provide one example each of an action/adventure movie set in the past, present and future and explain why each film worked well (or not) in its particular era. What elements would have to have been changed in order for it to be successful in a different time period?

3. Given the choice of being a pirate, an archaeologist or an explorer, which would you most like to be and what would be your quest?

TAKING A PAGE FROM REAL LIFE

The term "cinema verite" refers to films that reflect reality sans the artistic frills of fiction. When filmmaking first began over a century ago, visionaries such as the Lumière Brothers and Thomas Edison experimented with the medium by taking pictures of ordinary people working in factories, getting on and off trains, eating their lunch or just taking strolls in the park. The ability to capture images for posterity quickly led to the concept of recording newsworthy events such as groundbreaking ceremonies, parades, ship christenings, and political stumping. Globetrotting travelers soon saw the glamour of "actualities" — the first form of travelogues that could introduce foreign landscapes and mysterious cultures to those who might never go there themselves.

The advent of regular newsreels to keep people informed, propaganda films to advance social and economic causes, and at-home interviews with luminaries du jour were the forerunners of today's documentaries. These are nonfiction works that seek to examine who we are as a society, record events of special interest, stir controversy, analyze the past, explain how things work, or just provide us an up close and personal look at some of our most popular icons.

Documentaries can be as simple as unscripted, man-on-the-street interviews about a school or community issue or as complex and multi-media as Ken Burns' various mini-series on topics such as the Civil War, jazz, the West and baseball. Film producers have also discovered that behind-the-scenes documentaries on how their movies were made — combined with director/star interviews — have the advantage of drawing as many curious viewers as those who bought tickets and saw the actual movies.

LOOK & LEARN

What would happen if a TV talk show host were able to invite the likes of Saint Thomas Aquinas, Susan B. Anthony, Shakespeare and Cleopatra to drop into his living room for coffee and chat about their lives? Such was the premise of the late Steve Allen's innovative series, *Meeting of Minds*, which aired from 1977-1981 and featured historic guests debating issues of the day, explaining how they chose their particular professions, and even arguing with each other about their respective approaches to life. While each of the actors was well versed on the factual elements of their characters' backgrounds, the entire thing was orchestrated in such a seamless way that it was impossible to tell how much was scripted and how much was improvisation.

BRAINSTORMERS

1. What is currently the most controversial subject at your school? Is it the cafeteria lunch menu, increased campus security, dress codes, gang violence, the transfer of a favorite teacher, drug use? Identify an issue and, in a 100-word essay, explain how you would go about developing a half-hour documentary on this subject.

2. A producer decides that *Meeting of Minds* was a great show and wants to bring it back. Your assignment is to pick the first four guests and decide what topic they should talk about which will guarantee fabulous ratings. Explain your rationale.

3. Your assignment is to do a ten-minute documentary on dating. Your instructions are that there will be no voice overs, no dialogue and no title cards. You are, however, permitted to use any visuals, any music of your choice and any contextual message. Describe how you would put this documentary together.

THE MAGIC OF ANIMATION

In 1928, a plucky little mouse with a helium-infused voice became not only an overnight celebrity but the icon of a future theme park that would become known as "The Happiest Place on Earth." Although we associate Mickey Mouse with the debut of modern animation, he was actually preceded by Gertie the Dinosaur (1914), Felix the Cat (1919), Oswald the Rabbit (1927) and a number of experimental shorts derived from animation's predecessor: the newspaper comic strips. These hand-drawn, frame by frame films were targeted to appeal to children but have evolved through the decades into a sophisticated, computer-generated style of storytelling with genres, dialogue, Oscar-winning scores, 3D perspectives and celebrity-voiced casts that have found a large fan base in adults.

Advancements in animation techniques have further allowed humans to enter and interact in the "cartoon" world (*Who Framed Roger Rabbit?*) as well as successively imbued animated figures with facial expressions, body language, texture and gaits that are uncannily comparable to their real-life counterparts (*Shrek*).

While not impossible to achieve, the tales of anthropomorphic characters (i.e., animals and objects that act like humans) would be challenging to carry off with real actors and real sets. Likewise, the ease with which animated characters can perform astonishing feats, change form/size/color at will, and survive outlandish stunts/falls/explosions would translate to enormous costs in a human equation. Even in those instances where animated works have successfully transitioned to the Broadway stage and ice rinks, we tend to become more conscious of the actor in a fur suit than empathetic to the personality and colorful world of the animal or object being portrayed.

LOOK & LEARN

To enhance your appreciation of this genre and its creative evolution, compare the animation techniques of each film in the first column with the corresponding film in the second column:

◦ *A Charlie Brown Christmas*	◦ *The Simpsons*
◦ *Mary Poppins*	◦ *Who Framed Roger Rabbit?*
◦ *Snow White and the Seven Dwarfs*	◦ *Shrek*
◦ *Mulan*	◦ *Princess Mononoke*
◦ *Rudolph the Red Nose Reindeer*	◦ *Wallace & Gromit: A Close Shave*
◦ *The Three Little Pigs*	◦ *Jakes! The Adventures of Piggley Winks*
◦ *Lady and the Tramp*	◦ *All Dogs Go to Heaven*
◦ *The Bugs Bunny Show*	◦ *Beavis and Butt-Head*
◦ *Fantasia*	◦ *Howl's Moving Castle*
◦ *The Flintstones*	◦ *The Incredibles*

BRAINSTORMERS

1. "Anime" is the term given to Japanese animation films, many of which revolve around themes of dark fantasy and science fiction and are featured as part of the Saturday morning cartoon lineup. In a 100-word essay, compare and contrast the story content, dialogue and characters of anime with American animated series.

2. You've been asked to do an animated sequel to *Pirates of the Caribbean: The Curse of the Black Pearl*. How would you portray Captain Jack Sparrow? What would be his most important power as an animated character? Explain in a 100-word essay how you'd use animation to accomplish something a film couldn't do.

3. Among the choices of *Alien*, *Master and Commander: The Far Side of the World* and *The Brothers Grimm*, which would be the best film to adapt as a full-length animated feature? Explain your answer in a 100-word essay.

MUSIC, MUSIC, MUSIC

Prior to "talkies," early films relied on music to evoke a mood for the audience. Have you ever thought of your favorite music videos as a form of film short? With the exception of those that are strictly the memorialization of an actual concert, many of them intercut visuals that supplement the lyrics by relating mini-stories about love, heartbreak, loneliness, injustice, triumph, etc. In the absence of onscreen dialogue between the characters represented, these follow what you already have learned about classic story structure with a beginning, middle and end, use minimal locations as a backdrop, and — like silent films — feature only a handful of recurring cast members. In addition, the settings are usually contemporary and invite the use of special effects such as dissolves, mirages, morphing, superimposing, color manipulation and animation.

For aspiring filmmakers, music videos represent a challenging opportunity to tell a simple story through a series of montages, the unifying thread of which is a vocal or instrumental selection of music. For fledgling musicians, collaboration with a screenwriter provides a unique calling card by which to attract new gigs and recording opportunities. For both parties, these can be launched as streaming videos on the Internet, a placement that has been known to not only build a fan base but also catch the eye of producers surfing for fresh material to promote.

As a screenwriter, you may even want to try your hand at developing your script concept as a full-length musical. While the expense of production can be significantly higher, it can also be rewarding if you have a good ear for telling an original story through song and dance.

LOOK & LEARN

There are a number of Internet websites that allow you to download music videos for free. These are updated regularly to include the works of emerging artists as well as the hottest releases from established groups. A sampling of these sites is included below:

- *www.findvideos.com*
- *www.artistdirect.com*
- *www.singingfool.com*
- *http://membrane.com/rombox/*
- *http://music.aol.com*

BRAINSTORMERS

1. What is your favorite piece of music? Is it classical, jazz, R&B, country western, rap? Imagine that a producer has asked you to make a music video of this piece. She would like you to tell a mini-story through the intercut visuals. In a 200-word essay, explain how you would go about doing this.

2. What is your favorite music video? Have you ever watched it with the sound off? Your assignment is to hit the "mute" button and watch the video from start to finish. You will then write a 100-word synopsis explaining the story that you saw unfold through the accompanying visuals.

3. You have decided to write a musical screenplay about your school. What would you call it? Who are the primary characters? Where do the scenes mostly take place? Oh, and tell us what the plot would be and why a musical would best capture the film's theme.

FAMILY FARE AND COMING OF AGE

Family-oriented fare has steadily been making a comeback to movie screens around the country. So, too, are films that feature teenagers just like you who are fast approaching the threshold of adulthood with impatience and/or trepidation. Even in contemporary plots, both types of films follow what is called the classic structure of *myth*, the cornerstone of man's relentless quest to find his rightful place in society and — at the same time — try to balance it against what he believes are the rightful leanings of his heart.

Throughout history this struggle has been conveyed through tales about rites of passage, legends about personal sacrifice for the good of the tribe and morality lessons regarding the inevitable transition of power from an elder generation to a younger one. The cyclical nature of mythical structure is such that the security of the family unit and the teachings of responsibility lay the foundation for independence, a freedom which will eventually compel the offspring to long for the stability that only a home and family of their own can satisfy. Within that framework are the rebellious challenges to the status quo. Whether the young protagonist manifests in the form of a lion cub disobeying his father's rules, a headstrong girl wanting to pursue a non-traditional career, or star-crossed lovers who have to meet on the sly because their families hate each other, these are timeless conflicts that hold the power to resonate with audiences of any era.

The longstanding advice that English teachers give to "write what you know" applies very well to the family/coming-of-age genre. After all, who knows your family better than you? And who but you better understands your feelings during the trial-and-error process of spreading your wings and learning to fly?

LOOK & LEARN

Family values and peer pressures take centerstage in the following selection of films:

- *American Graffiti*
- *Grease*
- *To Sir, With Love*
- *Bend It Like Beckham*
- *Breaking Away*
- *Little Women*
- *The Breakfast Club*
- *Sixteen Candles*
- *Dead Poets Society*
- *13 Going on 30*
- *Freaky Friday*
- *The Member of the Wedding*

Family relationships are also popular fare for television:

- *Happy Days*
- *Family Ties*
- *The Wonder Years*
- *Malcolm in the Middle*
- *7th Heaven*
- *Dawson's Creek*
- *Gilmore Girls*
- *The Cosby Show*

BRAINSTORMERS

1. In a 300-word essay, compare and contrast any family TV series produced prior to the 1970s with any family series produced after 2000. How do these portrayals reflect families in real life? What do you think they will be like in the year 2050?

2. If you could trade your immediate relatives for one week for any of the TV families listed above, which one would it most likely be and why? The second part of this assignment is to write a 100-word synopsis describing an episode that revolves around your inclusion in this fictional tableau.

3. What is the one thing that you are most dreading when you officially become an adult? What is the basis for your anxiety? Write a three-page scene in which your protagonist has this same fear and is confiding it to his or her best friend. Next, write a three-page scene in which the anxiety is being expressed to a parent.

GENRE IS A REFLECTION OF ATTITUDE AND INTENTION

The word "camping" carries different meanings for different people. For someone who puts in sixty-plus hours a week in a skyscraper, camping represents a welcome respite from the pressures of Corporate America. For a kid, camping offers the chance to eat gooey S'mores, sleep outside, and tell ghost stories around a campfire. For nature lovers, it's an opportunity to be at one with flora and fauna. And to people like me — for whom "roughing it" means that there's no place to plug in my curling iron — camping is an invitation that will always be declined in favor of the nearest Ritz Carlton.

I use this analogy to show how the attitude you have toward your subject matter can be expressed to an audience through your choice of genre. Whatever genre you choose to emphasize will set the tone of the film and, thus, assist your intention of scaring, amazing, delighting or disturbing your viewers. To accomplish this, genres are used in three ways: (1) playing to formula' (2) introducing variation; and (3) defying convention.

A genre that plays to formula (boy meets girl/loses girl/gets girl back) creates a comfort level that satisfies an audience's need for the familiar. A genre that introduces variation (boy meets girl/loses girl/girl joins Mafia) creates surprise, controversy, shock and sadness. Genres that defy convention by mixing multiple styles (cowboy meets alien slasher/falls in love/solves high-tech crime) or attempting to maintain neutrality (guy sits on bench for two hours doing nothing) either fail to attract a market or are unique enough to become a cult classic. Certainly there's no better example of the latter than the comedy/horror/musical/sci-fi/romance/fantasy *The Rocky Horror Picture Show*, which debuted way back in 1975 and still sells out every performance.

LOOK & LEARN

Let's get back to camping. Figuratively, of course. Compare and contrast the genres of each of the following "summer camp" films. What opinions or attitudes did the writers have toward the subject of adventures in the great outdoors?

- *The Parent Trap*
- *Friday the 13th*
- *Bless the Beasts and the Children*
- *Meatballs*
- *Camp Nowhere*
- *Bloody Murder*
- *Magic Rock*
- *Bug Juice* (TV series)

BRAINSTORMERS

1. What genres of films do you tend to gravitate toward the most? In a 100-word essay, describe how your answer reflects your attitude and approach toward life.

2. Your assignment is to set a meeting between two people in a cemetery. Describe what elements (lighting, sound, special effects, props) you would incorporate to make this scene (1) a comedy; (2) a thriller; (3) a romance; (4) an action/adventure; (5) sci-fi; (6) a documentary.

3. *Life is Beautiful* and *Schindler's List* deal with the same topic — the Holocaust — through the use of two radically different genres. In a 100-word essay, discuss how both films celebrate the perseverance of the human spirit. How do these films respectively reflect the attitudes of directors Benigni and Spielberg?

ELVIS MAY HAVE LEFT THE BUILDING BUT HIS HEIRS ARE ALIVE AND KICKING

So here's a great idea, you think: Paris Hilton wakes up one day and discovers she's totally broke. Not wanting to let on to her partying pals, she decides to rob a bank. After all, she rationalizes, she'd never be considered a suspect if everyone still thought she was rich. Cool idea? It is until you hire a blond starlet look-alike and tell her she's playing a character named Paris Hilton. The real Paris, to say the least, would not be amused and probably hire real attorneys to sue you for lots of real money.

Given the often reckless way that today's celebrities enjoy making their private lives an open book, writers sometimes make the mistake of believing that this means their personalities, exploits and public disclosures can all be used for free in a work of fiction. Fueling this belief is the ongoing sighting of "dead celebrities" hawking soft drinks and snacks in commercial advertising — a marvel of technology that allows vintage clips to be seamlessly stitched into a gimmicky, modern context. No shortage of lawsuits abound where the heirs feel the reputation of the deceased has been compromised.

While none of this is to say that you can *never* make someone famous a character in your story, acquiring the legal rights to do so can often be cost-prohibitive to anyone but a major producer. The exception, of course, would be historical figures who have been dead for at least a century and preferably longer. Napoleon, for instance. Or Columbus.

Even if you're writing something that casts a living icon in a truly favorable light you think they'd really like, the bottom line is that you still need their permission to do it. After all, would you want someone stealing who *you* are and making a profit from it without asking you first if it was okay? I wouldn't think so.

LOOK & LEARN

Robert Zemekis, an associate of Steven Spielberg's, is an example of someone with access to the financial clout to resurrect whomever he wants for the purpose of an entertaining film. In 1994, he did exactly that with *Forrest Gump*, the story of a dense but likeable lad who unwittingly influences American pop culture and literally crosses paths with Elvis, three presidents and even John Lennon. A pricey production? Most definitely.

Does Hollywood ever do things on the cheap? That's the comedic premise of *Bowfinger* in which Steve Martin (as a desperate director) discovers that superstar Kit Ramsey (Eddie Murphy) has a dimwitted double. Justifying his strategy with silly lines like, "Did you know that Tom Cruise didn't know he was in that vampire movie until three months later?", Bowfinger sets out to shoot an entire film that banks on the doofy twin's ignorance and the arrogant Ramsey's lack of awareness he's being stalked.

BRAINSTORMERS

1. Let's go back to the Paris Hilton bank robber story. What changes would you need to make to her persona that would significantly distinguish the fictional invention from the nonfiction reality and, thus, avoid a potential lawsuit?

2. Technology is rapidly advancing to the point that deceased stars who never acted opposite each other can now be resurrected through computer generated imagery and be "cast" in new films. Write a 300-word essay that either argues *in favor* of the creativity this will allow screenwriters or *against* the practice on the grounds that the rights of the deceased will be compromised.

3. In a 100-word essay, explain what a parody is and how its use in TV comedy skits sidesteps the rules of acquiring formal permission from the people being portrayed.

RULES OF THE (FORMATTING) GAME

On dark and stormy nights, my husband and I will often pull out the Scrabble board and see if we can beat our prior scores. They're generally pretty high, owing to the fact that over the years we've come up with variations that include the use of state abbreviations, proper names, foreign nouns and the liberty to remove any tile that's already been played and replace it with a new one (as long as it still spells something). And hey, if you can use all the words in any given turn in a sentence and deliver it with a funny accent, you get 100 extra points. (As you can guess, we're very good at entertaining ourselves.) Suffice it to say, however, it precludes us from ever engaging in Scrabble matches with anyone who doesn't share our adventurous penchant to make the game more interesting. Even if — in our opinion — our version is better, diehard Scrabble fans would probably not be amused and refuse to embrace our originality.

This same rigidity can be said of prospective agents, directors and producers. Even though they know the content of each submission will be different, they demand a standard of uniformity in every presentation: the same font, the same margins, the same paper stock, etc. Stifling as these rules may seem in a venue as creative as film, they are actually to the writer's benefit and allow for a fair and unbiased evaluation of the work. What this means is that if you decide to ignore the rules and print your script in a neon green **Braggadocio** 16-point font on yellow onionskin paper and put it in a gold lamé three-ring binder so that you will stand out from the crowd, the good news is that you will get their attention. The bad news is that it will shout in capital letters that you don't know how to play by the rules and that your script is not worth their time.

LOOK & LEARN

Throughout this book, you've had a chance to download screenplays and familiarize yourself with proper film lingo and page layout. You've probably also noticed that not all of these scripts are consistent. Where the screenwriter is also the director/producer (James Cameron, for example), more liberties tend to be taken because the story is already a "done deal," not an unsolicited work to be pitched by a newcomer. If you have a commercial software program such as Final Draft, the mechanics of proper formatting are taken care of for you. If you're "winging it" with Word, however, there are plenty of online sites to help you set your margins, learn when to use caps and how to transition from one scene to the next. Here are a few to bookmark:

- *www.scriptologist.com*
- *www.storysense.com*
- *www.hollywoodlitsales.com*
- *www.breakingin.net*

BRAINSTORMERS

1. Haiku is a very structured form of Japanese poetry. After you have paid a visit to *www.toyomasu.com/haiku* and understand the five-seven-five syllabic rhythm and inclusion of a season, write a haiku poem on why you want to be a screenwriter.

2. Select a story from today's newspaper and, using correct format, write a two-page scene in which your protagonist, a reporter, is interviewing of one of the participants.

3. You're an agent who has received a handwritten script on binder paper, full of typos. The plot really has a lot of promise but the writer needs to understand why scripts have to follow proper format and be error-free. Write this person a diplomatic one-page letter explaining what needs to be fixed prior to resubmission.

BULLETPROOFING YOUR SCRIPT

Someone you've really been wanting to go out with for a long time has finally noticed that you exist and asks you for a date on Saturday night. You're really jazzed and spend most of the day deciding on just the right outfit, styling your hair and maybe even getting a manicure. When he shows up (an hour and a half late), you notice that he's wearing dirty clothes, an untucked shirt, smells as if he hasn't bathed recently, and calls you by the wrong name. He also announces that he didn't bring any money and so you'll be paying for both of your dinners and the movie.

One would hope at this point that — no matter how much of a hottie you think he is — you'd have the good sense to tell him to go away and not come back until he's presentable and worthy of your time. Interestingly, directors, producers and agents feel the same way about messy, error-riddled scripts that are accompanied by hand-scrawled cover letters that misspell their names. There may be a great idea — or a stellar personality — lurking behind the untidy presentation but why would anyone spend time digging it out if *no* time was apparently spent in making a polished appearance?

The most common mistakes that screenwriters make in their submissions are:

- Poor proofreading (don't rely entirely on spellcheck or your own eyes!)
- Descriptions and dialogue typed in CAPS, **boldface** or underlined.
- Incorrect fonts (use Courier 12 pt.) and excessive parentheticals.
- Lengthy descriptions and sidebar/footnote explanations by the author.
- Margins that deviate from standard formatting.
- Handwritten scripts, color ink, color paper, artwork or casting advice.
- Cover letters that are over-inflated ("This is the next *Gone With the Wind*"), whiney ("My doctor said it would help my self-esteem if you bought this script"), arrogant ("You haven't had a hit film in years") or inappropriately personal, ("Hi, George! How's it going at Skywalker Ranch these days?").

LOOK & LEARN

There's just no explaining sometimes why those who work hard at their craft are passed up for success by clueless rubes who just happen to stumble into the right situation at the right time. For veteran screenwriter Charlie Kaufman, portrayed by Nicholas Cage in *Adaptation*, he simply can't fathom why his twin brother, Donald — a man with absolutely no screenwriting experience or talent — is suddenly able to sell his first project for a million dollars. Charlie, meanwhile, is struggling to adapt a plotless novel about orchids and becomes increasingly vexed with Donald's nonstop chatter and advice about "the industry." *Adaptation* is an interesting take on the axiom that Hollywood doesn't know what it's looking for until it actually shows up. Film history, after all, is replete with examples of novices like Donald who simply got lucky. Luck, however, is no substitute for professionalism, perseverance and respecting the rules of the game.

BRAINSTORMERS

1. If you don't belong to one already, start a screenwriting group. This forum will allow everyone to have their scripts read aloud (a good way to catch dialogue and accent inconsistencies) as well as proofread each other's work prior to submission.

2. Good grammar and punctuation are just as critical in your presentation as perfect spelling and an expansive vocabulary. Go to *www.nonstopenglish.com* and start taking some of the tests. This is also a good website to bookmark as you prepare for college entrance exams.

3. Sometimes the best way to strengthen your own proofreading skills is to critique the scripts of others. Go to *www.zoetrope.com* and join in to get constructive (and free!) feedback on your film shorts and feature-length projects.

WHAT'S MINE IS MINE

Imagine that you just finished knitting a beautiful sweater with an original design and ask a stranger to try it on. The stranger immediately runs off with it. Shortly thereafter, you hear the news that the stranger is not only telling people it's hers but is also bragging that she knit the whole thing herself. What's your recourse? Well, unless a lot of people *saw* you knitting it or you had the foresight to sew a "Handcrafted By" label in it when you were done, your originality and ownership may be difficult to prove.

The same thing is true of screenplays. In a perfect world, you'd be able to send out copies of your script to interested parties and never have to worry about piracy. Unfortunately, this isn't a perfect world. Prospective producers are just as scared of authors suing them for stealing/modifying their ideas (e.g., Steven Spielberg is still dealing with lawsuits regarding *E.T.*) as authors are nervous about someone ripping them off. To that end, most production companies, screenplay contests and even script consultants insist that a screenplay be properly registered with one of the following agencies prior to submission in order to establish ownership and date of completion:

- U.S. Copyright Office — *www.copyright.gov*
- Writers Guild of America — *www.wga.org*
- Protect Rite — *www.protectrite.com*
- Write Safe — *www.writesafe.com*

Even when your script is registered, always exercise good judgment when you start sending it out. Specifically:

- Always send a copy, never your one and only original.
- Never send a script unless it has been requested.
- Keep accurate records of when the script was sent and to whom.
- Unless it's a contest fee, never pay a producer or agent to read your work.
- Never put the registration number or symbol © on your title page or script itself.

LOOK & LEARN

Failure to give proper credit where credit is due on intellectual properties such as stories can be a costly lesson. Eddie Murphy learned this in 1988 when he didn't acknowledge Art Buchwald as his co-writer in the comedy *Coming to America*. It was a mistake that resulted in the courts ordering Murphy to give Buchwald 19% of the film's earnings.

More recently, Joel Turnipseed (a former Marine who authored a novel called *Baghdad Express*) became embroiled in controversy over the inspiration for *Jarhead*. Although the director and screenwriter maintain that their film was adapted from Anthony Swofford's memoirs of the first Gulf War, Turnipseed has cited entire scenes and events from the pages of his book. The filmmakers' rebuttal? "These are stories that are held in common by all Marines." In other words, the similarities are "just coincidence."

BRAINSTORMERS

1. What steps can you take to protect your script while it is still a work in progress? Explain in a 100-word essay.

2. If you wanted to adapt a story written by someone else and turn it into a short film, explain how you would go about determining whether the material was still protected by copyright or had fallen into what is called "public domain."

3. The "poor man's copyright" — mailing something to yourself and not opening the envelope — is a legitimately recognized method of establishing the completion date of a manuscript without having to pay a fee. Identify at least three reasons why this particular method is faulty.

SCREENWRITING COMPETITIONS

Writing contests of any kind can be a great barometer of how you're doing in the skills department. While the receipt of recognition is always a wonderful incentive to do "more of same," the receipt of feedback can be just as valuable in identifying what you need to work on in order to reach the winners' circle. And, unlike scattergun pitches to production companies and agents that may or may not generate a response, the administrators and judges of screenplay contests *are* looking for new works to read.

The trick is in knowing which ones are real and which ones are bogus. Yes, it's true, the Internet has become a lucrative feeding ground for entrepreneurs who have absolutely no connection to the film industry but who are more than happy to take your entry fees (and your ideas!) for their own use. Fortunately, there's also a proliferation of screenwriting chat rooms and websites such as Movie Bytes (*www.moviebytes.com*) that allow you to look before you leap into a competition that may not be legit.

For those contests that *are* on the level, the bottom line is to **follow the rules to the letter!** Insider tip: Scripts that don't do this are automatically eliminated and not read. Among the most common mistakes are:

- Providing more than has been requested (or the wrong genre!).
- Not attaching the required fees.
- Improperly formatted scripts.
- Late submissions.
- Revised versions of the originally submitted material.
- More typos than you can shake a stick at.

LOOK & LEARN

There are a number of screenwriting contests that are specifically targeted to high school and college students. Here's a starter list:

- ACE High School Script Contest
- Great American Student Film Festival & Short Screenplay Competition
- Samuel Goldwyn Writing Awards
- UCLA Extension Screenwriting Competition
- Studio Academy
- Nicholls Screenwriting Fellowships

The fees and entry requirements for these and other annual competitions can be found at *www.moviebytes.com*. In addition, trade magazines such as *Scr(i)pt*, *MovieMaker*, and *Writer's Digest* provide announcements of contest information and regional film festivals.

BRAINSTORMERS

1. Have you completed your short or feature film? Go to the Movie Bytes website listed above and identify at least three screenwriting contests for which your project would qualify.

2. In a 100-word essay, identify how you would go about researching the legitimacy of a screenplay competition that you have never heard of.

3. Is your school film class looking for new projects? Develop and publicize a screenwriting contest for your fellow students that establishes ground rules which are consistent with the time constraints, locations and technical resources currently available to the "producers."

FAST PITCH

In earlier chapters, you learned the importance of being able to craft snappy loglines and a concise synopsis that doesn't meander. Both of these skills will serve you well when it comes to actually pitching your project to a prospective producer or film agent for consideration. Pitching a concept or an actual script is either done in writing in the form of a cover letter or in a live presentation which is called a pitch session. In both cases, you only have a very short amount of time to get someone excited enough about your proposal to want to read the whole thing.

A written pitch should ideally be no more than one typed page and address (1) what the story is about; (2) who the target audience is; and (3) your particular qualifications to write this material. It should always be directed to a specific person (as opposed to "Dear Universal Studios") and include a self-addressed, stamped envelope as well as pertinent contact information. *Never* send the complete script unless you have been requested to do so and *never* follow up with pesky phone calls asking why they haven't made a decision yet.

Live pitches are either as a result of the follow up to an inquiry letter or are an "open call" invitation connected to a screenwriters' conference. The time to make your pitch is usually limited to three to ten minutes so don't be late in keeping your appointment! Listen carefully to any criticism you receive but *never* engage in argument about the merits of your script. Always inquire whether you can follow up with new proposals, remember the names of the people with whom you have spoken and be sure to thank them for their time and consideration, even if the outcome was not exactly what you were hoping for.

LOOK & LEARN

The Script-Selling Game by Kathie Fong Yoneda is a wonderful and insightful primer for anyone who wants to understand the nuts and bolts of how a script wends its way through the Hollywood system. Of particular interest are her chapters on how to take a meeting with moguls, industry buzzwords to commit to memory, establishing ongoing relationships with the people who can give your script the greenlight and the importance of creating networking opportunities for yourself. Available through amazon.com, this is one book that needs to belong on every aspiring young screenwriter's bookshelf.

BRAINSTORMERS

1. Write a one-page cover letter pitching your current project. Give copies of this inquiry letter to ten different people and ask them to provide feedback on how it could be improved.

2. You have been invited to a pitch session and will have three minutes to "sell" the listeners on your idea. Practice by setting an egg timer and keep rehearsing until you can deliver your entire spiel before the buzzer goes off.

3. Set up a mock pitch session with your fellow screenwriting students. As a collective group, you will have the opportunity to ask questions of each aspiring screenwriter. This rehearsal process will not only prepare you for the types of questions a prospective production company might ask but groom you for the challenge of keeping cool under fire, listening attentively, and applying the feedback to your script as well as preparation for your *next* pitch session.

SCREENWRITER'S ETIQUETTE

Screenwriting is a job. As such, it needs to be approached like any other job. Specifically:

- Learning how to do the required tasks.
- Seeking out potential employers.
- Preparing for — and acing — an interview.
- Getting hired.
- Staying hired.

To accomplish these objectives, however, requires two things that have not only fallen by the wayside in our school system but have slipped in emphasis for society as well. Courtesy and respect — the hallmark of good breeding a century ago — have taken a distant backseat to arrogance, greed, dishonesty, and a belief in entitlement. That these messages are repeatedly reinforced by actors, pro athletes and corporate America has given many young people the impression that being rude or self-centered is the only way to get ahead.

If you want to be a successful screenwriter, you need to know that movies are the collaborative effort of many people. Yes, you're the one with the story. That story, however, can't be told without someone to direct it, financiers to pay for it, actors to act in it, camera people to film it, costume designers to supply the clothes, musicians to write a score, advertising execs to create a buzz, and an audience to walk through the doors. And hey, even those teens behind the counter selling popcorn, sodas, and Milk Duds are part of what will make a night at the theater a wonderfully enjoyable event.

Be nice to all of them. Respect that their views may be different from yours. Observe the courtesy of being punctual, returning phone calls and not trashing your competition. Word travels fast in this town. Make sure it's nothing less than favorable.

LOOK & LEARN

The Player is a must-see for anyone considering a career in the film business. In this dark comedy about Hollywood sleaze, an arrogant screener for a film studio has gleefully let power go to his head. His callous rejection of a recent script, however, has now garnered postcard death threats from the writer. Unfortunately, the screener has no idea which of the multitude of writers he's rejected is behind a plot to kill him. His desperation to get to the truth subsequently leads to him murdering the wrong man and then trying to cover it up, a scenario that provides the real author with enough blackmail to raise the stakes.

BRAINSTORMERS

1. A small, independent production company has just optioned your first screenplay for $1,000 and you're pretty excited. You're even more excited when, the following week, you get a call from James Cameron who offers you ten times that amount for the very same script. What would you do?

2. You hear about a producer who is looking for a family script about an immigrant family from India. A fellow student you really hate has a script that would be perfect for it. Would you let your enemy in on this opportunity or keep it to yourself? What if the person with the script was your best friend?

3. You've been collaborating on a script with another writer. It's been going okay but you've just met someone you think would be more fun to work with. How would you handle this situation? Keep in mind that you have both contributed equally to the script and, thus, have an equal ownership in it.

YOU HATE ME. YOU REALLY HATE ME.

As the writing of this book draws to a close, I'm reading an email that says, "I am going to quit writing forever because I'm tired of people picking on me and hurting my feelings. I want to be rich and famous and live in Hollywood but it's taking way too long. Why should I keep putting myself through this if I'm never going to get anywhere?"

Oy. How do you reply to someone who — at sixteen — has decided to give up on something that a scant six months ago was "the only thing I've ever wanted to do"? A part of me wants to take a page from Cher in *Moonstruck* and tell her to "Snap out of it!" Another part of me wants to relate stories of my own tortured teen years and close with the plucky epilogue, "But see? Everything all worked out just fine."

And then there's the part somewhere in the middle that knows I need to tell her exactly what I'm about to say to any of you who might someday come to me with the same doubts about whether you should keep writing or just settle for a dull and uninspired life selling appliances somewhere in New Jersey.

The upside to being any kind of artist — be it writing, music, painting — is that you have the freedom to wildly unleash your imagination, march to your own drummer and vividly color outside the lines. Unlike the precision of math and science, there is no "right" answer, only the answer that feels right to *you* in expressing your idea.

The downside to being an artist, however, lies in the multitude of people who think there *is* a right answer and, accordingly, deem that *you*, the artist, have no clue what it is. Why these multitudes always manage to gravitate to jobs like editors, agents, publishers, producers and newspaper critics is anyone's guess.

The truth is, not everyone is going to like what you do. Not everyone is going to hate it, either. The operative word, of course, is *It*, not *You*. The majority of the time, the people to whom you submit your work wouldn't recognize you if they passed you on the street. All they know is the product you've put under their nose and whether it smells like a hit. If it smells like something else, it doesn't mean you should take it personally. It just means you should send them something new or simply acknowledge that maybe they aren't the best match for what you want to express.

You need to remember that this is a fickle and mercurial business. What doesn't sell this week could be in enormous demand by the end of next month. On the flip side, you could get lucky the first time out and then be inundated with enough rejection letters the following year to wallpaper the bathroom. Becoming successful — at *anything* — is often a matter of outlasting the competition. It's also a matter of "knowing what you don't know" and endeavoring to master it so your skill level will improve.

The point of all of this is that you've chosen to be a writer because you love to write, not because writing represents a cool way to get rich and famous. Many rich and famous writers, in fact, have said throughout their careers that even if no one ever paid them a cent, they'd continue to write because it's something that has been coursing through their veins for as long as they can remember. They also recognize the brutally subjective nature of this craft. If ten different people have ten enormously different opinions about a particular work, that just goes to prove it. On the other hand, if all ten people pick out exactly the *same* flaws, I've always found it helpful to revisit the material and try to learn from what they unanimously felt could be improved.

As you've probably noticed by now, this chapter — the final one in our journey — breaks the format you've been used to. There's no Look & Learn nor are there the usual trio of Brainstormer exercises. There is, however, a request I'm going to make of any of you who ever feel the same sense of defeat as the young girl who wrote to tell me she thinks her screen career is over before she's even old enough to vote. Here it is: If at such point you ever decide to quit, I want you to write me an essay entitled, "The Ten Reasons I Really Hate Writing and Would Never Want to Do It for a Living" and send it to *authorhamlett@cs.com.*

If your essay is compelling enough to convince me that you don't love writing anymore, I'll respect your decision and, reluctantly, I promise to let you go. On the other hand, if you find that it's hard to come up with even *one* good reason to stop believing in the dream of making movie magic, I want you to use the same email address to write and tell me when you've had your first success.

And you know what *I'll* say?

> CHRISTINA
> (with a wink)
> I told you so.

> FADE TO BLACK

FILMOGRAPHY ·

TITLE OF PRODUCTION	YEAR	STARRING
Abbott and Costello Meet Frankenstein	1948	Bud Abbott, Lou Costello
Adaptation	2002	Nicholas Cage, Meryl Streep, Chris Cooper
The Adventures of Pluto Nash	2002	Eddie Murphy, Randy Quaid
The Adventures of Robin Hood	1938	Errol Flynn, Olivia de Havilland, Basil Rathbone, Claude Raines
The African Queen	1951	Humphrey Bogart, Katharine Hepburn
The Alamo	1960	John Wayne, Richard Widmark, Laurence Harvey
Alias (TV series)	2001- 2006	Jennifer Garner, Victor Garber, Michael Vartan
All the President's Men	1976	Dustin Hoffman, Robert Redford
The Amazing Race (TV series)	2001-	*Non-actors in unscripted performance*
American Beauty	1999	Kevin Spacey, Annette Bening, Thora Birch
American Graffiti	1973	Richard Dreyfuss, Ron Howard, Harrison Ford, Cindy Williams
The American President	1995	Michael Douglas, Annette Bening, Michael J. Fox, Martin Sheen
Andromeda (TV series)	2000-2005	Kevin Sorbo
Animal Crackers	1930	The Marx Brothers

TITLE OF PRODUCTION	YEAR	STARRING
Antz	1998	*Voices of* Woody Allen, Dan Aykroyd, Anne Bancroft, Danny Glover
Attack of the 50 Foot Woman	1958	Allison Hayes, William Hudson, Yvette Vickers
Attack of the Crab Monsters	1957	Richard Garland, Pamela Duncan, Russell Johnson
The Avengers	1998	Ralph Fiennes, Uma Thurman
The Aviator	2004	Leonardo DiCaprio, Cate Blanchett, Alan Alda
Babe	1995	James Cromwell, *Voice of* Christine Cavanaugh
Back to the Future	1985	Michael J. Fox, Christopher Lloyd
Bad Santa	2003	Billy Bob Thornton
The Bad Seed	1956	Patty McCormack, Nancy Kelly
Barefoot in the Park	1967	Robert Redford, Jane Fonda
Battlestar Gallactica (mini-series)	2003	Edward James Olmos, Mary McDonnell
A Beautiful Mind	2001	Russell Crowe, Ed Harris, Jennifer Connelly
Beauty and the Beast	1991	*Voices of* Robby Benson, Paige O'Hara, Angela Lansbury, Jerry Orbach
Beavis and Butt-Head (TV series)	1993-1997	*Voices of* Mike Judge, Tracy Grandstaff, Adam Welsh
Before Sunrise	1994	Ethan Hawke, Julia Delpy
Being There	1979	Peter Sellers, Shirley MacLaine
The Bellboy	1960	Jerry Lewis
Bend It Like Beckham	2002	Parminder K. Nagra, Keira Knightley
Bewitched	2005	Nicole Kidman, Will Farrell

TITLE OF PRODUCTION	YEAR	STARRING
Big	1988	Tom Hanks, Elizabeth Perkins, Robert Loggia
Big Jake	1971	John Wayne, Richard Boone, Bruce Cabot
Billy Elliot	2000	Jamie Bell, Jean Heywood, Gary Lewis, Nicola Blackwell
The Birds	1963	Tippi Hedren, Rod Taylor, Suzanne Pleshette, Jessica Tandy
The Blair Witch Project	1999	Heather Donahue, Joshua Leonard, Michael Williams
Blazing Saddles	1974	Gene Wilder, Cleavon Little, Slim Pickens
Bless the Beasts and the Children	1971	Bill Mumy, Barry Robins, Jesse White, David Ketchum
Bloody Murder	2000	Jessica Morris, Peter Guillemette
The Bourne Identity	2002	Matt Damon, Chris Cooper, Franka Potente
Bowfinger	1999	Steve Martin, Eddie Murphy
Braveheart	1995	Mel Gibson, Patrick McGoohan, Sophie Marceau
Breakfast at Tiffany's	1961	Audrey Hepburn, George Peppard, Patricia Neal
The Breakfast Club	1985	Emilio Estevez, Molly Ringwald, Ally Sheedy
Breaking Away	1979	Dennis Quaid, Dennis Christopher, Barbara Barrie
Breaking Home Ties	1987	Jason Robards, Eva Marie Saint, Doug McKeon
Brian's Song	1971	James Caan, Billie Dee Williams
Bride and Prejudice	2004	Martin Henderson, Aishwarya Rai
Bridget Jones' Diary	2001	Renee Zellweger, Colin Firth, Hugh Grant
The Brothers Grimm	2005	Matt Damon, Heath Ledger

TITLE OF PRODUCTION	YEAR	STARRING
The Brothers McMullen	1995	Jack Mulcahy, Edward Burns, Mike McGlone
Bug Juice (TV Series)	1998-2000	*Middle school documentary*
The Bugs Bunny Show (TV series)	1960-1968	*Voices of* Mel Blanc, Jim Backus, Arthur Q. Bryan
Butch Cassidy and the Sundance Kid	1969	Paul Newman, Robert Redford, Katharine Ross
The Butterfly Effect	2004	Ashton Kutcher, Amy Smart
Camp Nowhere	1994	John Putch, Peter Scolari, Jonathan Jackson
Cape Fear	1991	Robert De Niro, Nick Nolte, Jessica Lange
Carrie	1976	Sissy Spacek, Amy Irving, John Travolta
Casablanca	1942	Humphrey Bogart, Ingrid Bergman
Catch Me If You Can	2002	Leonardo DiCaprio, Tom Hanks
Cellular	2004	Kim Basinger, Chris Evans, William H. Macy
Chapter Two	1979	James Caan, Marsha Mason
Chariots of Fire	1981	Ben Cross, Ian Charleson
Charlie & the Chocolate Factory	2005	Johnny Depp, Freddie Highmore
A Charlie Brown Christmas	1965	*Voices of* Bill Melendez, Peter Robbins, Tracy Stratford
Charlie's Angels	2000	Cameron Diaz, Drew Barrymore, Lucy Liu
Charmed (TV Series)	1998-2006	Shannon Doherty, Alyssa Milano, Holly Marie Combs
The Cherokee Kid	1996	Sinbad, Gregory Hines, James Coburn, Burt Reynolds
Cheyenne Autumn	1964	Richard Widmark, Karl Malden, Ricardo Montalban

TITLE OF PRODUCTION	YEAR	STARRING
Chitty Chitty Bang Bang	1968	Dick Van Dyke, Sally Ann Howes. Lionel Jeffries
Citizen Kane	1941	Orson Welles, Joseph Cotten, Agnes Moorehead
Clerks	1994	Brian O'Halloran, Jeff Anderson
The Client	1994	Susan Sarandon, Tommy Lee Jones, Brad Renfro
Close Encounters of the Third Kind	1977	Richard Dreyfuss, Francois Truffaut, Teri Garr
Clueless	1995	Alicia Silverstone, Paul Rudd, Brittany Murphy
The Color Purple	1985	Danny Glover, Whoopi Goldberg, Oprah Winfrey
Come Blow Your Horn	1963	Frank Sinatra, Lee J. Cobb, Jill St. John
Coming to America	1988	Eddie Murphy, Arsenio Hall, James Earl Jones
Conan the Barbarian	1982	Arnold Schwarzenegger, James Earl Jones, Max von Sydow
Constantine	2005	Keanu Reeves, Rachel Weisz
The Cosby Show (TV series)	1984-1992	Bill Cosby, Phylicia Rashad, Malcolm Jamal-Warner
Covington Cross (TV Series)	1992	Nigel Terry, Cherie Lunghi
The Crimson Pirate	1952	Burt Lancaster, Eva Bartok
Crossing Jordan (TV series)	2001-	Jill Hennessy, Miguel Ferrer
Crouching Tiger, Hidden Dragon	2000	Chow Yun-Fat, Michelle Yeoh, Ziyi Zhang
The Crying Game	1992	Forrest Whitaker, Stephen Rea, Miranda Richardson
Dances with Wolves	1990	Kevin Costner, Mary McDonnell
Daredevil	2003	Ben Affleck, Jennifer Garner, Colin Farrell

TITLE OF PRODUCTION	YEAR	STARRING
Dave	1993	Kevin Kline, Sigourney Weaver, Frank Langella, Ben Kingsley
Dawson's Creek (TV series)	1998-2003	James Van Der Beek, Katie Holmes, Joshua Jackson
Dead Again	1991	Kenneth Branagh, Emma Thompson, Andy Garcia
Dead Poets Society	1989	Robin Williams, Robert Sean Leonard, Ethan Hawke
Death of a Salesman	1951	Fredric March, Mildred Dunnock, Cameron Mitchell
The Devil's Own	1997	Harrison Ford, Brad Pitt
Dharma and Greg (TV series)	1997-2002	Jenna Elfman, Thomas Gibson
Dial M for Murder	1954	Grace Kelly, Ray Milland
Die Hard	1988	Bruce Willis, Alan Rickman, Bonnie Bedelia
Do the Right Thing	1989	Spike Lee, Ossie Davis, Ruby Dee, Danny Aiello
Double Indemnity	1944	Fred MacMurray, Barbara Stanwyck
Dr. Jekyll & Mr. Hyde	1931	Fredric March, Miriam Hopkins
Doctor Zhivago	1965	Omar Sharif, Julie Christie, Geraldine Chaplin, Rod Steiger, Alec Guiness
Dracula	1931	Bela Lugosi, Helen Chandler
Dragonheart	1996	Dennis Quaid, David Thewlis, Julie Christie, *Voice of* Sean Connery
Drumline	2002	Nick Cannon, Zoe Saldana, Orlando Jones
Duck Soup	1933	The Marx Brothers

TITLE OF PRODUCTION	YEAR	STARRING
Dumb and Dumber	1994	Jim Carrey, Jeff Daniels
El Mariachi	1992	Carlos Gallardo, Consuelo Gomez
Elektra	2005	Jennifer Garner
ER (TV series)	1994-	Noah Wyle, Sherry Stringfield, Maura Tierney, Ming-Na, Goran Visnjic
Everybody Loves Raymond (TV series)	1996-2005	Ray Romano, Patricia Heaton, Peter Boyle, Doris Roberts, Brad Garrett
Excalibur	1981	Nigel Terry, Helen Mirren, Nicol Williamson, Cherie Lunghi
The Exorcist	1973	Ellen Burstyn, Max von Sydow, Linda Blair
Family Ties (TV series)	1982-1989	Michael J. Fox, Meredith Baxter, Michael Gross
Fantasia	1940	*Animation*
Fantastic Four	2005	Ioan Gruffudd, Jessica Alba, Chris Evans, Michael Chiklis
Fatal Attraction	1987	Michael Douglas, Glenn Close
Ferris Bueller's Day Off	1986	Matthew Broderick, Alan Ruck, Mia Sara
A Few Good Men	1992	Jack Nicholson, Tom Cruise, Demi Moore
The Fifth Element	1997	Bruce Willis, Gary Oldman
Fight Club	1999	Brad Pitt, Helena Bonham Carter, Meat Loaf
Finding Nemo	2003	*Voices of* Albert Brooks, Ellen DeGeneres

TITLE OF PRODUCTION	YEAR	STARRING
Finding Neverland	2004	Johnny Depp, Kate Winslet, Julie Christie
The Flintstones (TV series)	1960-1966	*Voices of* Alan Reed, Mel Blanc, Jean Vander Pyl, Bea Benaderet
Forrest Gump	1994	Tom Hanks, Sally Field, Gary Sinise
Frances	1982	Jessica Lange, Sam Shepard
Frankenstein	1931	Boris Karloff, Colin Clive
Freaky Friday	2003	Jamie Lee Curtis, Lindsay Lohan, Mark Harmon
Friday the 13th	1980	Kevin Bacon, Betsy Palmer
Friends (TV series)	1994-2004	Jennifer Aniston, Courtney Cox, Lisa Kudrow, Matt LeBlanc, Matthew Perry, David Schwimmer
The Fugitive	2000	Harrison Ford, Tommy Lee Jones
Galaxy Quest	1999	Tim Allen, Sigourney Weaver, Alan Rickman
Gandhi	1982	Ben Kingsley, Candice Bergen, Edward Fox, John Gielgud
Ghost	1990	Patrick Swayze, Demi Moore, Whoopi Goldberg
Ghostbusters	1984	Bill Murray, Sigourney Weaver, Dan Aykroyd, Rick Moranis
Gilligan's Island (TV series)	1964-1967	Bob Denver, Alan Hale, Jr., Jim Backus
Gilmore Girls (TV series)	2000-	Lauren Graham, Alexis Bledel
Girl, Interrupted	1999	Winona Ryder, Angelina Jolie

TITLE OF PRODUCTION	YEAR	STARRING
Gladiator	2000	Russell Crowe
Going in Style	1979	George Burns, Art Carney, Lee Strasberg
Gone with the Wind	1939	Clark Gable, Vivien Leigh, Leslie Howard, Olivia DeHavilland
The Good, the Bad and the Ugly	1966	Clint Eastwood, Lee Van Cleef, Eli Wallach
Grease	1978	John Travolta, Olivia Newton-John
The Great Escape	1963	Steve McQueen, Richard Attenborough, Charles Bronson, David McCallum
Groundhog Day	1993	Bill Murray, Andie MacDowell
Happy Days (TV series)	1974-1984	Ron Howard, Henry Winkler, Tom Bosley
Harold and Maude	1971	Ruth Gordon, Bud Cort
Harry Potter and the Prisoner of Azkaban	2004	Daniel Radcliffe, Maggie Smith, Gary Oldman
Harry Potter and the Sorcerer's Stone	2001	Daniel Radcliffe, Maggie Smith, Richard Harris
Heaven Can Wait	1978	Warren Beatty, Julie Christie, Charles Grodin, James Mason
Herbie, Fully Loaded	2005	Lindsay Lohan, Michael Keaton
Here on Earth	2000	Chris Klein, Leelee Sobieski, Josh Hartnett
High Noon	1952	Gary Cooper, Grace Kelly
Highlander	1986	Sean Connery, Christopher Lambert, Roxanne Hart

TITLE OF PRODUCTION	YEAR	STARRING
Highlander 3	1994	Christopher Lambert, Mario Van Peebles, Deborah Kara Unger
Home for the Holidays	1995	Holly Hunter, Robert Downey, Jr., Anne Bancroft
The Hours	2002	Nicole Kidman, Meryl Streep, Julianne Moore
Howl's Moving Castle	2004	*Voices of* Emily Mortimer, Christian Bale, Lauren Bacall, Billy Crystal
Hullabaloo (TV series)	1965-1966	Patrick Adiarte, Brian Epstein, Donna McKechnie
The Hunt for Red October	1990	Sean Connery, Alec Baldwin
I Am Sam	2001	Sean Penn, Michelle Pfeiffer, Dakota Fanning, Dianne Wiest
I Dream of Jeannie (TV series)	1965-1970	Larry Hagman, Barbara Eden, Bill Daily
In the Heat of the Night	1967	Sidney Poitier, Rod Steiger
The Incredibles	2004	*Voices of* Craig T. Nelson, Holly Hunter, Samuel L. Johnson
The Inspector General	1949	Danny Kaye, Walter Slezak, Elsa Lanchester
The Interpreter	2005	Nicole Kidman, Sean Penn
Invaders from Mars	1953	Helena Carter, Arthur Franz, Jimmy Hunt
Invasion of the Body Snatchers	1956	Kevin McCarthy, Dana Winter, Carolyn Jones
The Island	2005	Ewan McGregor, Scarlett Johansson

TITLE OF PRODUCTION	YEAR	STARRING
It Came from Outer Space	1953	Richard Carlson, Barbara Rush
It's a Wonderful Life	1946	James Stewart, Donna Reed, Lionel Barrymore
Jakers! The Adventures of Piggley Winks (TV series)	2003-2005	*Voices of* Maile Flanagan, Russi Taylor, Tara Strong, Mel Brooks
Jarhead	2005	Peter Sarsgaard, Jake Gyllenhaal
Jason and the Argonauts	1963	Todd Armstrong, Nancy Kovack, Gary Raymond
Jaws	1975	Roy Scheider, Robert Shaw, Richard Dreyfuss
Jeepers-Creepers	2001	Jonathan Breck, Justin Long, Gina Phillips
JFK	1991	Kevin Costner, Gary Oldman
Joan of Arc	1948	Ingrid Bergman, J. Carrol Naish, Jose Ferrer
Joan of Arcadia (TV series)	2003-2005	Amber Tamblyn, Joe Mantegna, Mary Steenburgen
Jumanji	1995	Robin Williams, Jonathan Hyde, Kirsten Dunst, Bonnie Hunt
Jurassic Park	1993	Sam Neill, Laura Dern, Jeff Goldblum, Richard Attenborough
Kate and Leopold	2001	Meg Ryan, Hugh Jackman
Kramer vs. Kramer	1979	Dustin Hoffman, Meryl Streep
La Femme Nikita	1990	Anne Parillaud, Jeanne Moreau
Lady and the Tramp	1955	*Voices of* Barbara Luddy, Larry Roberts

TITLE OF PRODUCTION	YEAR	STARRING
Ladyhawke	1985	Matthew Broderick, Rutger Hauer, Michelle Pfeiffer
Lara Croft, Tomb Raider	2001	Angelina Jolie
Laura	1944	Gene Tierney, Dana Andrews, Clifton Webb, Vincent Price
A League of Their Own	1992	Tom Hanks, Geena Davis, Madonna
Legally Blonde	2001	Reese Witherspoon, Luke Wilson, Victor Garber
Lemony Snicket's A Series of Unfortunate Events	2004	Jim Carrey, Jude Law, Billy Connolly, Meryl Streep
Lethal Weapon	1987	Mel Gibson, Danny Glover
Life Is Beautiful	1997	Roberto Benigni, Nicoletta Braschi
Lifeboat	1944	Tallulah Bankhead, Walter Slezak, William Bendix
The Lion in Winter	1968	Katharine Hepburn, Peter O'Toole, Anthony Hopkins, Timothy Dalton
The Lion King	1994	*Voices of* Matthew Broderick, James Earl Jones, Jeremy Irons
Little Women	1994	Winona Ryder, Gabriel Byrne, Kirsten Dunst, Susan Sarandon
Lord of the Flies	1963	James Aubrey, Tom Chapin, Hugh Edwards
The Lord of the Rings: The Fellowship of the Ring	2001	Elijah Wood, Ian McKellan, Viggo Mortensen, Liv Tyler
The Lord of the Rings: The Return of the King	2003	Elijah Wood, Sean Astin, Viggo Mortensen

TITLE OF PRODUCTION	YEAR	STARRING
Lost in Yonkers	1993	Richard Dreyfuss, Mercedes Ruhl, Irene Worth
The Lost World	1960	Michael Rennie, Jill St. John, David Hedison, Claude Raines, Fernando Lamas
A Lot Like Love	2005	Ashton Kutcher, Amanda Peet
The Love Bug	1968	Dean Jones, Michele Lee
Mad Hot Ballroom	2005	*NYC public school kids (documentary)*
Madagascar	2005	*Voices of* Ben Stiller, Chris Rock, David Schwimmer, Jada Pinkett Smith
Magic Rock	2001	Miko Hughes, Bradley Gallo, Jimmy McQuaid
The Magnificent Seven	1960	Yul Brynner, Steve McQueen, Charles Bronson
Malcolm in the Middle (TV series)	2000-2006	Jane Kaczmarek, Frankie Muniz
The Man Who Shot Liberty Valance	1962	John Wayne, Jimmy Stewart, Vera Miles, Lee Marvin
The Manchurian Candidate	1962	Frank Sinatra, Angela Lansbury, Laurence Harvey
Marathon Man	1976	Dustin Hoffman, Laurence Olivier
Mary Poppins	1964	Julie Andrews, Dick Van Dyke
Master and Commander: The Far Side of the World	2003	Russell Crowe, Paul Bettany
The Matrix	1999	Keanu Reeves, Laurence Fishburn, Carrie-Anne Moss
Meatballs	1979	Bill Murray, Kate Lynch
Meet Joe Black	1998	Anthony Hopkins, Brad Pitt

TITLE OF PRODUCTION	YEAR	STARRING
Meeting of Minds (TV series)	1977-1981	Steve Allen, Jayne Meadows
The Member of the Wedding	1952	Ethel Waters, Julie Harris, Brandon De Wilde
Memento	2000	Guy Pearce, Carrie-Anne Moss
Men in Black	1997	Tommy Lee Jones, Will Smith
Men of Honor	2000	Cuba Gooding, Jr., Robert De Niro, Charlize Theron
Million Dollar Baby	2004	Clint Eastwood, Hilary Swank, Morgan Freeman
Minority Report	2002	Tom Cruise, Max von Sydow
Mission Impossible	1996	Tom Cruise, Jon Voight
Monsters, Inc.	2001	*Voices of* John Goodman, Billy Crystal
Moon Over Parador	1988	Richard Dreyfuss, Raul Julia, Sonia Braga
Moonstruck	1987	Cher, Nicholas Cage, Danny Aielo, Olympia Dukakis
Mork and Mindy (TV series)	1978-1982	Robin Williams, Pam Dawber
Mr. Smith Goes to Washington	1939	James Stewart, Jean Arthur, Claude Raines
Mrs. Doubtfire	1993	Robin Williams, Sally Field, Harvey Fierstein
Mulan	1998	*Voices of* Ming-Na, Harvey Fierstein, Eddie Murphy
The Mummy	1999	Brendan Fraser, Rachel Weisz
My Favorite Martian (TV series)	1963-1966	Ray Walston, Bill Bixby
National Treasure	2004	Nicholas Cage, Sean Bean, Jon Voight
A Nightmare on Elm Street	1984	Robert Englund

TITLE OF PRODUCTION	YEAR	STARRING
Norma Rae	1979	Sally Field, Ron Leibman, Beau Bridges
North by Northwest	1959	Cary Grant, Eva Marie Saint, James Mason
Not Another Teen Movie	2001	Chris Evans, Eric Christian Olsen, Chyler Leigh, Mia Kirshner
The Odd Couple (TV Series)	1970-1975	Tony Randall, Jack Klugman
Oh, God!	1977	George Burns, John Denver, Teri Garr
The Omen	1976	Gregory Peck, Lee Remick, David Warner
On Golden Pond	1981	Henry Fonda, Katharine Hepburn, Jane Fonda
One Flew Over the Cuckoo's Nest	1975	Jack Nicholson, Louise Fletcher
101 Dalmatians	1996	Glenn Close, Jeff Daniels, Joely Richardson
One on One (TV series)	2001-	Flex Alexander, Kyla Pratt
Ordinary People	1980	Donald Sutherland, Mary Tyler Moore, Timothy Hutton
Pale Rider	1985	Clint Eastwood, Michael Moriarty, Carrie Snodgress
The Parent Trap	1961	Hayley Mills, Maureen O'Hara, Brian Keith
The Party	1968	Peter Sellers, Claudine Longet, Steve Franken
The Patriot	2000	Mel Gibson, Heath Ledger, Joely Richardson
Pay It Forward	2000	Kevin Spacey, Helen Hunt, Haley Joel Osment, Jay Mohr
The Perfect Storm	2000	George Clooney, Mark Wahlberg, Diane Lane
Peter Pan	2003	Jason Issacs, Jeremy Sumpter, Rachel Hurd-Wood, Lynn Redgrave

TITLE OF PRODUCTION	YEAR	STARRING
Philadelphia	1993	Tom Hanks, Denzel Washington
Phone Booth	2002	Colin Farrell, Kiefer Sutherland, Katie Holmes
Pinocchio	2002	Roberto Benigni
Pirates of the Caribbean	2003	Johnny Depp, Orlando Bloom, Keira Knightley
Planet of the Apes	1968	Charlton Heston, Kim Hunter, Roddy McDowell
The Player	1992	Tim Robbins, Peter Gallagher, Greta Scacchi
Pleasantville	1998	Tobey Maguire, Reese Witherspoon
The Polar Express	2004	Tom Hanks
The Princess Bride	1987	Cary Elwes, Robin Wright, Chris Sarandon
The Princess Diaries	2001	Julie Andrews, Anne Hathaway
Princess Mononoke	1997	*Voices of* Billy Crudup, Minnie Driver, Billy Bob Thornton, Jada Pinkett-Smith
Psycho	1960	Janet Leigh, Anthony Perkins
The Punk	1993	Charlie Creed-Miles, Vanessa Hadaway
Pygmalion	1938	Leslie Howard, Wendy Hiller
Radio	2003	Cuba Gooding, Jr., Ed Harris, Alfre Woodard
Ragtime	1981	James Cagney, Elizabeth McGovern, Howard E. Rollins, Jr.
Raiders of the Lost Ark	1981	Harrison Ford, Karen Allen
Rain Man	1988	Dustin Hoffman, Tom Cruise

TITLE OF PRODUCTION	YEAR	STARRING
Ransom	1996	Mel Gibson, Gary Sinise, Rene Russo
Rebecca	1940	Laurence Olivier, Joan Fontaine, Judith Anderson
Reunion (TV series)	2005-2006	Dave Annable, Alexa Davalos, Will Estes, Sean Faris, Chyler Leigh, Amanda Righetti, Mathew St. Patrick
Reversal of Fortune	1990	Jeremy Irons, Glenn Close, Ron Silver
Rio Bravo	1959	John Wayne, Dean Martin, Ricky Nelson
Risky Business	1983	Tom Cruise, Rebecca DeMornay
Robin and Marian	1976	Sean Connery, Audrey Hepburn, Robert Shaw, Richard Harris
Robin Hood, Prince of Thieves	1991	Kevin Costner, Morgan Freeman, Mary Elizabeth Mastrantonio, Alan Rickman
Robin Hood: Men in Tights	1993	Cary Elwes, Richard Lewis, Roger Rees
Robots	2005	*Voices of* Robin Williams, Halle Berry, Mel Brooks, Drew Carey
Rocky	1976	Sylvester Stallone, Talia Shire, Carl Weathers, Burgess Meredith
The Rocky Horror Picture Show	1975	Tim Curry, Susan Sarandon, Barry Bostwick
Romance	1913/1920/1930	*Stage play* (1913) *and silent film* (1920) *starred* Doris Keane; 1930 *film starred* Greta Garbo

TITLE OF PRODUCTION	YEAR	STARRING
Romancing the Stone	1984	Michael Douglas, Kathleen Turner
Romeo and Juliet	1954	Laurence Harvey, Susan Shentall, Sebastian Cabot
Rudolph the Red Nosed Reindeer	1964	*Voices of* Burl Ives, Billie Mae Richards, Paul Soles
Run Lola Run	1998	Franka Potente, Moritz Bleibtreu
Rush Hour, Rush Hour 2	1998/2001	Jackie Chan, Chris Tucker
S1mOne	2002	Al Pacino, Rachel Roberts
Sabrina, The Teenage Witch (TV Series)	1996-2003	Melissa Joan Hart, Caroline Rhea, Beth Broderick
Saint Ralph	2004	Adam Butcher, Campbell Scott, Shauna MacDonald
Save the Last Dance	2001	Julia Stiles, Sean Patrick Thomas
Say Anything	1989	John Cusack, Ione Skye, John Mahoney
Schindler's List	1993	Liam Neeson, Ben Kingsley, Ralph Fiennes
Scream/Scream 2	1996	David Arquette, Neve Campbell, Courtney Cox
Scrubs (TV series)	2001 -	Zach Braff, Sarah Chalke, Donald Faison
Seabiscuit	2003	Jeff Bridges, Tobey Maguire
The Searchers	1956	John Wayne, Jeffrey Hunter, Natalie Wood
Searching for Bobby Fischer	1993	Max Pomeranc, Joe Mantegna, Laurence Fishburn, Joan Allen, Ben Kingsley
Secret Window	2004	Johnny Depp, John Turturro, Mario Bello, Timothy Hutton

TITLE OF PRODUCTION	YEAR	STARRING
Seinfeld (TV series)	1990-1998	Jerry Seinfeld, Julia Louis-Dreyfus, Michael Richards, Jason Alexander
7th Heaven (TV series)	1996-2006	Stephen Collins, Catherine Hicks
Shakespeare in Love	1998	Joseph Fiennes, Gwyneth Paltrow, Judi Dench, Colin Firth
Shane	1953	Alan Ladd, Jean Arthur, Van Heflin, Jack Palance, Brandon De Wilde
Shanghai Knights	2003	Jackie Chan, Owen Wilson
She's All That	1999	Freddie Prinze, Jr., Rachel Leigh Cook
The Shining	1980	Jack Nicholson, Shelley Duvall, Danny Lloyd
Shrek and Shrek 2	2001/2004	*Voices of* Mike Myers, Eddie Murphy, Cameron Diaz, Antonio Banderas
Sidekicks	1992	Chuck Norris, Beau Bridges, Jonathan Brandis, Joe Piscopo
The Silence of the Lambs	1991	Anthony Hopkins, Jodie Foster
Silkwood	1983	Meryl Streep, Kurt Russell, Cher
The Simpsons (TV series)	1989-	*Voices of* Dan Castellaneta, Julie Kavner, Nancy Cartwright
Sister Act	1992	Whoopi Goldberg, Maggie Smith, Kathy Najimy, Harvey Keitel

TITLE OF PRODUCTION	YEAR	STARRING
The Sisterhood of the Traveling Pants	2005	Amber Tamblyn, Alexis Bledel, America Ferrera, Blake Lively
Sixteen Candles	1984	Molly Ringwald, Michael Schoeffling
The Sixth Sense	1999	Bruce Willis, Haley Joel Osment
Sky High	2005	Kurt Russell, Kelly Preston, Michael Angarano
Sleeping with the Enemy	1991	Julia Roberts, Patrick Bergen
Sleepless in Seattle	1993	Tom Hanks, Meg Ryan
Sliding Doors	1998	Gwyneth Paltrow, John Hannah, John Lynch
Snow White and the Seven Dwarfs	1937	*Voices of* Adriana Caselotti, Lucille La Verne, Roy Atwell
Something's Gotta Give	2003	Jack Nicholson, Diane Keaton
Somewhere in Time	1980	Christopher Reeve, Jane Seymour, Christopher Plummer
Spaceballs	1987	Mel Brooks, Rick Moranis, Bill Pullman, Daphne Zuniga
Speed	1994	Sandra Bullock, Keanu Reeves
Spider-Man 2	2004	Tobey Maguire, Kirsten Dunst, Alfred Molina
Spy Game	2001	Robert Redford, Brad Pitt
Star Trek	1966	William Shatner, Leonard Nimoy, DeForest Kelley

TITLE OF PRODUCTION	YEAR	STARRING
Star Wars	1977	Mark Hamill, Harrison Ford, Carrie Fisher, Alec Guinness
Stealth	2005	Josh Lucas, Jessica Biel, Jamie Foxx
The Sting	1973	Paul Newman, Robert Redford, Robert Shaw
Strangers on a Train	1951	Farley Grander, Ruth Roman, Robert Walker, Leo G. Carroll
Superman	1978	Christopher Reeve, Margot Kidder, Gene Hackman, Marlon Brando
The Sure Thing	1985	John Cusack, Daphne Zuniga, Anthony Edwards
Survivor (TV series)	2000-	*Non-actors in unscripted performance*
10 Things I Hate About You	1999	Heath Ledger, Julia Stiles
The Texas Chainsaw Massacre	1974	Marilyn Burns, Paul A. Partain, Allen Danziger
That 70's Show (TV series)	1998-2006	Ashton Kutcher, Laura Prepon, Topher Grace, Danny Masterson
Them!	1954	James Whitmore, James Arness, Edmund Gwenn
There's Something About Mary	1998	Cameron Diaz, Matt Dillon, Ben Stiller
The Three Little Pigs	1933	*Voices of* Pinto Colvig, Dorothy Compton, Mary Moder, Billy Bletcher
Third Rock from the Sun (TV series)	1996-2001	John Lithgow, Jane Curtain, Kristen Johnston, French Stewart, Joseph Gordon-Leavitt

TITLE OF PRODUCTION	YEAR	STARRING
13 Going on 30	2004	Jennifer Garner, Mark Ruffalo
Three Men & a Baby	1987	Tom Selleck, Ted Danson, Steve Guttenberg
Titanic	1997	Leonardo DiCaprio, Kate Winslet, Billy Zane, Kathy Bates, Victor Garber
To Kill a Mockingbird	1962	Gregory Peck
To Sir, With Love	1967	Sidney Poitier
Tombstone	1993	Kurt Russell, Val Kilmer, Sam Elliott, Bill Paxton
Tootsie	1982	Dustin Hoffman, Jessica Lange, Teri Garr, Charles Durning
Tortilla Soup	2001	Hector Elizondo, Raquel Welch, Elizabeth Peña
Toy Story	1995	*Voices of* Tom Hanks, Tim Allen
TRON	1982	Jeff Bridges, David Warner, Bruce Boxleitner
True Lies	1994	Arnold Schwarzenegger, Jamie Lee Curtis
12 Angry Men	1957	Henry Fonda, Martin Balsam, Lee J. Cobb
12 Monkeys	1995	Bruce Willis, Brad Pitt
24 (TV series)	2000-	Kiefer Sutherland
2001: A Space Odyssey	1968	Keir Dullea, Gary Lockwood
The Unknown	1927	Lon Chaney, Joan Crawford
Valiant	2005	*Voices of* Ewan McGregor, Tim Curry, John Cleese

TITLE OF PRODUCTION	YEAR	STARRING
Van Helsing	2004	Hugh Jackman, Kate Beckinsale, Richard Roxburgh
The Verdict	1982	Paul Newman, Jack Warden, James Mason
Veronica Mars (TV series)	2004 -	Kristen Bell, Percy Daggs III
Vertigo	1958	James Stewart, Kim Novak
A Walk in the Clouds	1995	Keanu Reeves, Aitana Sanchez-Gijon, Anthony Quinn
Wallace & Gromit: A Close Shave	1995	*Voices of* Peter Sallis, Anne Reid
War of the Worlds	2005	Tom Cruise, Dakota Fanning
The Way We Were	1973	Robert Redford, Barbra Streisand
The West Wing (TV series)	1999 -2006	Martin Sheen, Stockard Channing, Allison Janney, John Spencer
What Dreams May Come	1998	Robin Williams, Cuba Gooding Jr., Annabella Sciorra, Max von Sydow
What Ever Happened to Baby Jane?	1962	Bette Davis, Joan Crawford
When Harry Met Sally	1989	Meg Ryan, Billy Crystal
While You Were Sleeping	1995	Sandra Bullock, Bill Pullman, Peter Gallagher
Who Framed Roger Rabbit?	1988	Bob Hoskins, Christopher Lloyd, *Voice of* Charles Fleischer
Who's That Girl?	1987	Madonna, Griffin Dunne
Will and Grace (TV series)	1998-2006	Eric McCormack, Debra Messing, Megan Mullally, Sean Hayes

TITLE OF PRODUCTION	YEAR	STARRING
Willy Wonka & the Chocolate Factory	1971	Gene Wilder, Jack Albertson, Peter Ostrum
Windtalkers	2002	Nicholas Cage, Adam Beach, Christian Slater, Roger Willie
Witness	1985	Harrison Ford, Kelly McGillis, Lukas Haas
The Wizard of Oz	1939	Judy Garland, Ray Bolger, Bert Lahr, Jack Haley
The Wolf Man	1941	Claude Rains, Ralph Bellamy, Bela Lugosi, Lon Chaney, Jr.
The Wonder Years (TV series)	1988-1993	Fred Savage, Ally Mills, Dan Lauria, Josh Saviano, Danica McKellar
X the Unknown	1956	Dean Jagger, Edward Chapman, Anthony Newley
Yentl	1983	Barbra Streisand, Mandy Patinkin, Amy Irving
You Never Can Tell	1951	Dick Powell, Peggy Dow, Charles Drake
You've Got Mail	1998	Meg Ryan, Tom Hanks
Young Frankenstein	1974	Gene Wilder, Peter Boyle, Marty Feldman, Teri Garr

RECOMMENDED READING

A Dictionary of American Idioms	Maxine Tull Boatner and John Edward Gates	Barron's Educational Series (1975)
American Given Names: Their Origin and History	George Rippey Stewart	Oxford University Press (1979)
Careers for your Characters	Raymond Obstfeld and Franz Neumann	Writer's Digest Books (2002)
Could It be a Movie? How to Get Your Ideas From Out of Your Head and Up on the Screen	Christina Hamlett	Michael Wiese Productions (2005)
How To Make a Movie for Under $800	Ken Costanza	Authorhouse (2004)
Idiom's Delight (Spanish, French, Italian, Latin)	Suzanne Brock	Times Books (1988)
Inner Drives: How To Write and Create Characters Using the Eight Classic Centers of Motivations	Pamela Jaye Smith	Michael Wiese Productions (2005)
New Dictionary of American Family Names	Elsdon C. Smith	Gramercy Publishing (1988)

Rewrites	Neil Simon	Simon and Schuster (1996)
ScreenTEENwriters: How Young Screenwriters Can Find Success	Christina Hamlett	Meriwether Publishing (2002)
The Complete Writer's Guide to Heroes and Heroines: Sixteen Master Archetypes	Tami D. Cowden, Caro LaFever, Sue Viders	Lone Eagle Publishing (2000)
The Script-Selling Game: A Hollywood Insider's Look at Getting Your Script Sold and Produced	Kathie Fong Yoneda	Michael Wiese Productions (2002)
The Secret Universe of Names: The Dynamic Interplay of Names and Destiny	Roy Feinson	The Overlook Press (2004)
The Talk Book: The Intimate Science of Communicating in Close Relationships	Gerald Goodman, PhD. And Glenn Esterly	Rodale Press (1988)

ABOUT THE AUTHOR

Former actress and director Christina Hamlett is a professional script coverage consultant and award-winning author whose credits to date include 24 books, 118 plays and musicals, 4 optioned films and screenwriting columns that appear regularly throughout the United States, United Kingdom, Canada, Australia and New Zealand.

Her degree in Communications from California State University, Sacramento led to assignments in all aspects of media, cable television and public relations, including the development of her own touring theater repertory company which she ran for eight years.

In addition to her work as a grants consultant for Young Filmmakers Academy and feature writer for the San Marino Tribune, she teaches online screenwriting classes as well as workshops around the country for writers of all ages. She is married to insurance industry executive Mark Webb and resides in Pasadena, California.

Christina can be reached for questions or script consultations via her office at *authorhamlett@cs.com.*

ABOUT THE AUTHOR'S ASSISTANT

Since first meeting Christina Hamlett at the Lyndon Institute, Nicholas Morgan has written several screenplays and continued his study of the craft. An avid reader and writer, he is interested in both film and narrative writing. For several years he served as staff writer for a popular teen entertainment website. He is currently a student at Concord Academy in Concord, Massachusetts and lives in southern Vermont.

MICHAEL WIESE PRODUCTIONS

Since 1981, Michael Wiese Productions has been dedicated to providing both novice and seasoned filmmakers with vital information on all aspects of filmmaking. We have published more than 70 books, used in over 500 film schools and countless universities, and by hundreds of thousands of filmmakers worldwide.

Our authors are successful industry professionals who spend innumerable hours writing about the hard stuff: budgeting, financing, directing, marketing, and distribution. They believe that if they share their knowledge and experience with others, more high quality films will be produced.

And that has been our mission, now complemented through our new web-based resources. We invite all readers to visit www.mwp.com to receive free tipsheets and sample chapters, participate in forum discussions, obtain product discounts — and even get the opportunity to receive free books, project consulting, and other services offered by our company.

Our goal is, quite simply, to help you reach your goals. That's why we give our readers the most complete portal for filmmaking knowledge available — in the most convenient manner.

We truly hope that our books and web-based resources will empower you to create enduring films that will last for generations to come.

Let us hear from you at anytime.

Sincerely,
Michael Wiese
Publisher, Filmmaker

www.mwp.com

8043

Cinematic Storytelling: *The 100 Most Powerful Film Conventions Every Filmmaker Must Know* / Jennifer Van Sijll / $24.95

Complete DVD Book, The: *Designing, Producing, and Marketing Your Independent Film on DVD* / Chris Gore and Paul J. Salamoff / $26.95

Complete Independent Movie Marketing Handbook, The: *Promote, Distribute & Sell Your Film or Video* / Mark Steven Bosko / $39.95

Could It Be a Movie?: *How to Get Your Ideas Out of Your Head and Up on the Screen* / Christina Hamlett / $26.95

Creating Characters: *Let Them Whisper Their Secrets* Marisa D'Vari / $26.95

Crime Writer's Reference Guide, The: *1001 Tips for Writing the Perfect Crime* Martin Roth / $20.95

Cut by Cut: *Editing Your Film or Video* Gael Chandler / $35.95

Digital Filmmaking 101, 2nd Edition: *An Essential Guide to Producing Low-Budget Movies* / Dale Newton and John Gaspard / $26.95

Digital Moviemaking, 2nd Edition: *All the Skills, Techniques, and Moxie You'll Need to Turn Your Passion into a Career* / Scott Billups / $26.95

Directing Actors: *Creating Memorable Performances for Film and Television* Judith Weston / $26.95

Directing Feature Films: *The Creative Collaboration Between Directors, Writers, and Actors* / Mark Travis / $26.95

Eye is Quicker, The: *Film Editing; Making a Good Film Better* Richard D. Pepperman / $27.95

Fast, Cheap & Under Control: *Lessons Learned from the Greatest Low-Budget Movies of All Time* / John Gaspard / $26.95

Film & Video Budgets, 4th Updated Edition Deke Simon and Michael Wiese / $26.95

Film Directing: Cinematic Motion, 2nd Edition Steven D. Katz / $27.95

Film Directing: Shot by Shot, *Visualizing from Concept to Screen* Steven D. Katz / $27.95

Film Director's Intuition, The: *Script Analysis and Rehearsal Techniques* Judith Weston / $26.95

Film Production Management 101: *The Ultimate Guide for Film and Television Production Management and Coordination* / Deborah S. Patz / $39.95

Filmmaking for Teens: *Pulling Off Your Shorts* Troy Lanier and Clay Nichols / $18.95

First Time Director: *How to Make Your Breakthrough Movie* Gil Bettman / $27.95

From Word to Image: *Storyboarding and the Filmmaking Process* Marcie Begleiter / $26.95

Hitting Your Mark, 2nd Edition: *Making a Life – and a Living – as a Film Director* Steve Carlson / $22.95

Hollywood Standard, The: *The Complete and Authoritative Guide to Script Format and Style* / Christopher Riley / $18.95

I Could've Written a Better Movie Than That!: *How to Make Six Figures as a Script Consultant even if You're not a Screenwriter* / Derek Rydall / $26.95

Independent Film Distribution: *How to Make a Successful End Run Around the Big Guys* / Phil Hall / $24.95

Independent Film and Videomakers Guide – 2nd Edition, The: *Expanded and Updated* / Michael Wiese / $29.95

Inner Drives: *How to Write and Create Characters Using the Eight Classic Centers of Motivation* / Pamela Jaye Smith / $26.95

I'll Be in My Trailer!: *The Creative Wars Between Directors & Actors* John Badham and Craig Modderno / $26.95

Moral Premise, The: *Harnessing Virtue & Vice for Box Office Success* Stanley D. Williams, Ph.D. / $24.95

Myth and the Movies: *Discovering the Mythic Structure of 50 Unforgettable Films* / Stuart Voytilla / $26.95

On the Edge of a Dream: *Magic and Madness in Bali* Michael Wiese / $16.95

Perfect Pitch, The: *How to Sell Yourself and Your Movie Idea to Hollywood* Ken Rotcop / $16.95

Power of Film, The Howard Suber / $27.95

Psychology for Screenwriters: *Building Conflict in your Script* William Indick, Ph.D. / $26.95

Save the Cat!: *The Last Book on Screenwriting You'll Ever Need* Blake Snyder / $19.95

Screenwriting 101: *The Essential Craft of Feature Film Writing* Neill D. Hicks / $16.95

Screenwriting for Teens: *The 100 Principles of Screenwriting Every Budding Writer Must Know* / Christina Hamlett / $18.95

Script-Selling Game, The: *A Hollywood Insider's Look at Getting Your Script Sold and Produced* / Kathie Fong Yoneda / $16.95

Selling Your Story in 60 Seconds: *The Guaranteed Way to get Your Screenplay or Novel Read* / Michael Hauge / $12.95

Setting Up Your Scenes: *The Inner Workings of Great Films* Richard D. Pepperman / $24.95

Setting Up Your Shots: *Great Camera Moves Every Filmmaker Should Know* Jeremy Vineyard / $19.95

Shaking the Money Tree, 2nd Edition: *The Art of Getting Grants and Donations for Film and Video Projects* / Morrie Warshawski / $26.95

Sound Design: *The Expressive Power of Music, Voice, and Sound Effects in Cinema* / David Sonnenschein / $19.95

Stealing Fire From the Gods, 2nd Edition: *The Complete Guide to Story for Writers & Filmmakers* / James Bonnet / $26.95

Storyboarding 101: *A Crash Course in Professional Storyboarding* James Fraioli / $19.95

Ultimate Filmmaker's Guide to Short Films, The: *Making It Big in Shorts* Kim Adelman / $16.95

What Are You Laughing At?: *How to Write Funny Screenplays, Stories, and More* / Brad Schreiber / $19.95

Working Director, The: *How to Arrive, Thrive & Survive in the Director's Chair* Charles Wilkinson / $22.95

Writer's Journey, – 2nd Edition, The: *Mythic Structure for Writers* Christopher Vogler / $24.95

Writer's Partner, The: *1001 Breakthrough Ideas to Stimulate Your Imagination* Martin Roth / $24.95

Writing the Action Adventure: *The Moment of Truth* Neill D. Hicks / $14.95

Writing the Comedy Film: *Make 'Em Laugh* Stuart Voytilla and Scott Petri / $14.95

Writing the Killer Treatment: *Selling Your Story Without a Script* Michael Halperin / $14.95

Writing the Second Act: *Building Conflict and Tension in Your Film Script* Michael Halperin / $19.95

Writing the Thriller Film: *The Terror Within* Neill D. Hicks / $14.95

Writing the TV Drama Series: *How to Succeed as a Professional Writer in TV* Pamela Douglas / $24.95

DVD & VIDEOS

Field of Fish: *VHS Video* Directed by Steve Tanner and Michael Wiese, Written by Annamaria Murphy / $9.95

Hardware Wars: *DVD* / Written and Directed by Ernie Fosselius / $14.95

Sacred Sites of the Dalai Lamas – DVD, The: *A Pilgrimage to Oracle Lake* A Documentary by Michael Wiese / $22.95